PRAYING
WITH MARY

Praying
With Mary

Msgr. David E. Rosage

LIVING FLAME PRESS
LOCUST VALLEY, N.Y. 11560

Third printing 1983

Cover Design: J.M. Thielen

All scripture quotations are from the New American Bible.

Nihil Obstat: Rev. Michael Savelesky, *Censor Librorum*
April 15, 1980

Imprimatur: The Most Rev. Lawrence H. Welsh, D.D.,
Bishop of Spokane, April 18, 1980

Published by: Living Flame Press/Box 74/Locust Valley,
N.Y. 11560

ISBN: 0-914544-31-4

Printed in the United States of America

Dedication

To Our Mother
To My Mother
To All Mothers

Contents

Introduction 9
How to Use This Book for Prayer. 13
A Flower Unfolds. 15
Our Solitary Boast. 19
Summit Meeting. 24
A Humble Heart Rejoices. 29
A Joyous Heart Sings. 34
Love Causes Pain. 38
Prayer Is the Key. 42
Sign of Contradiction. 46
Escape to Egypt. 50
A Painful Search. 54
An Expectant Faith. 58
An Extravagant Response. 63
Word Power. 68
His Devoted Disciple. 73
An Anguished, Joyful Encounter. 78
A Mother's Fidelity. 83
Pieta 87
Sealed With a Stone. 92
Faith's Reward. 96

Gathered in My Name. 100
Sharing a Mother. 104
Non-Stop Flight to Heaven. 108
Mary, Queen of Heaven. 113
Mother of the Church. 118

Introduction

We are deeply grateful to our mothers for bringing us from our earliest years to a knowledge and love of our Father in heaven. How patiently and perseveringly they taught us to verbalize, in simple childlike language, our love and thanks to our good God. These first instructions were followed by the formulae of prayer which we learned by rote memory.

Our own prayer and our relationship with God was deepened and enriched by the example of our parents, especially by their faith and trust in God, their hope and love, and their own commitment to a life of prayer. We will be eternally grateful to our parents.

As we matured in our personal relationship with the Holy Trinity we discovered another Mother who would lead us into a more meditative and a more contemplative relationship with the Father, Son and Holy Spirit.

Mary is an ideal exemplar of prayer. Her life of prayer challenges us. Mary lived a life of prayer.

Her whole life, perfectly in tune with God's will, was her prayer. It was her lifestyle.

The scriptural references to Mary in the New Testament are sparse. This is understandable since the purpose of the evangelists was to tell us who Jesus is, what he did and said. Even though the references to Mary are few and brief, she, nevertheless, is woven like a golden thread through the whole New Testament.

It is interesting to note how many of these few references to Mary tell us something about her prayer life. What an ideal prayer posture we find in Mary's surrendering herself unconditionally and wholeheartedly to God when the angel announced to her God's divine plan. How generous her response: "I am the servant of the Lord. Let it be done to me as you say" *Luke 1:38.*

Mary's sheer joy at the goodness of God finds expression in her prayer of praise and thanksgiving, the Magnificat. We rejoice daily with Mary and with the whole Church as we pray this Canticle with Mary.

When the shepherds came at the invitation of the angels, they saw and they understood. Mary was overjoyed at their simple, but sturdy faith. Her prayer became contemplative: "Mary treasured all these things and reflected on them in her heart" *(Luke 2:19).*

Twelve years later we again discover Mary contemplating God's mysterious design. When

Joseph and Mary found Jesus "in the temple sitting in the midst of the teachers, listening to them and asking them questions. . . they were astonished. . . . " "His mother meanwhile kept all these things in memory" *(Luke 2:46ff)*. Thus Mary leads us into contemplative prayer.

At the wedding feast in Cana of Galilee, Mary teaches us the value of the prayer of petition. How simple her prayer: "They have no more wine." How confident she was of being heard for she turned to the waiters with the instruction: "Do whatever he tells you" *(John 2:1ff)*.

Mary is also our paragon of praying with Scripture. She was open and receptive to God's Word at all times, permitting it to inspire, change and transform her. Jesus was pointing to Mary's praying with Scripture when he announced: "Rather, blest are they who hear the word of God and keep it" *(Luke 11:28)*.

Under the cross Mary's prayer was one of total oblation to the Father in union with her own Divine Son. Her prayer was wordless, but the offering of her self is the heart of prayer.

We find Mary once again in the role of intercessor in the Upper Room after the Ascension. "Together they devoted themselves to constant prayer. There were some women in their company, and Mary the mother of Jesus, and his brothers" *(Acts 1:14)*. How fervently Mary must have prayed for the outpouring of the Holy Spirit on the infant Church. She knew from her own personal experience the presence and the power of the Holy Spirit.

These vignettes of Mary's prayer life serve as a model to give us the inspiration and motivation we need in our own life of prayer. We are encouraged to pray always. Mary shows us the way since prayer was her lifestyle.

In the pages which comprise this book, we can visit with Mary at various stages of her life and beg her to teach us how to pray.

How to Use This Book for Prayer

1. Settle into a relaxed position in your favorite place for prayer. "Be still and know that I am God" *(Psalm 46:11)*.

2. Ask Mary to help you enter into a prayer posture of quiet listening with your whole being.

3. Read the suggested Scripture passage slowly and reflectively. Read the thoughts in each chapter, remembering that these are but pathways into prayer.

4. Reread the Scripture slowly, pausing at a word or thought when your heart bids you to listen. Simply rest there.

5. Bask in the sunshine of God's presence, permitting his divine life to mold and transform your heart.

6. If you become distracted, quietly within your heart repeat a word which might have surfaced during moments of prayer, e.g. "Jesus" or "Mary" or "Thank You" or any other word which comes to you.

7. Do not end your prayer abruptly, but slowly

and calmly pray the "Hail Mary" or the "Memorare." Pray with your heart rather than your lips.

A Flower Unfolds

Luke 1:26-38

In the scriptural account of the Annunciation we find many levels of mystery. It is one of the unique events of salvation history.

The first awesome phase of this mystery is God's eagerness to communicate himself to us, his creatures, through his Son Jesus. St. John summarizes the merciful, compassionate love of the Father for us in one brief statement:

> "Yes, God so loved the world
> that he gave his only Son,
> that whoever believes in him may not
> die but may have eternal life"
> (John 3:16).

The second level of that mystery is the infinite love which Jesus has, not only for his Father, but for each one of us. That love could not be satisfied until he had given himself totally and entirely. St. Paul reminds us of the limitlessness of

15

Jesus' love: "Rather, he emptied himself and took the form of a slave being born in the likeness of men" *(Philippians 2:7).*

Did not Jesus himself remind us: "As the Father has loved me, so I have loved you" *(John 15:9)?* And in that same setting of the Last Supper, Jesus repeated the affirmation of his love for us: "There is no greater love than this: to lay down one's life for one's friends" *(John 15:13).*

It was his great love for the Father which prompted Jesus to say: ". . . I have come to do your will, O God" *(Hebrews 10:7).* Jesus also assured his followers: "Doing the will of him who sent me and bringing his work to completion is my food" *(John 4:34).*

How aptly in a popular song we speak of love as "ah sweet mystery of life."

The third phase of mystery surrounding this event is God's unique communication with Mary through his messenger, the angel Gabriel. God's requesting Mary's cooperation is enveloped in mystery.

Understandably Mary was startled at this divine manifestation in human history. A thousand thoughts must have tumbled through her mind as she pondered Gabriel's words.

How could she explain this mysterious, divine phenomenon? According to the endless and intricate interpretations of the law, and the cultural mentality of her own people, all that Mary could expect was total rejection by her family, by the villagers of Nazareth and even by Joseph, the man she loved so dearly.

In spite of the avalanche of rejection which would come her way, the voice of God had spoken. She asked only one question. It was not a question of hesitation, but one of clarification: "How can this be since I do not know man?" In other words how am I to fulfill God's divine plan? Mary's sinlessness had already removed all pride, self-centeredness and all the other hindrances which prevent us from giving ourselves completely to God. Her intense love of God compelled her to give herself without reserve.

How memorable her words of acquiescence: "I am the servant of the Lord. Let it be done to me as you say" *(Luke 1:38)*.

Like her Son, Mary could say with the psalmist: "To do your will, O my God, is my delight" *(Psalm 40:9)*. These words reveal the mentality and the mindset of Mary. Mary believes; she trusts, she gives in and her resolve becomes a lifelong commitment.

The fourth phase of mystery surrounds our own life. Life is a continual dying to self, to our pride, our self-centeredness, our ambition, our own will. Life is the total surrender of ourselves in love to our Father in heaven. St. Paul calls it the folly of the cross.

Jesus prepares us for the mystery of this kind

of discipleship: "Whoever wishes to be my follower must deny his very self, take up his cross each day, and follow in my steps. Whoever would save his life will lose it, and whoever loses his life for my sake will save it" *(Luke 9:23-24)*.

Theologians explain purgatory as a state in which this dying to self and this giving of ourselves in love to God continues in the afterlife if we have not fully done so while here on earth.

Like Mary, our life must always be an act of faith — every moment of it. We cannot understand all that happens in our life. We must simply believe, and we must trust our Father who loves us with an infinite love.

Mary gave her unconditional yes to the Father and it brought her through the primitive simplicity of Bethlehem, the lonely exile of Egypt, the dire poverty of Nazareth on to the dreadful pain of Calvary. Nevertheless her trust never failed because her love never diminished.

The greatest gift we can give to the Lord is the gift of ourselves. Be assured that Mary's faith and trust will sustain our faith and trust. Be assured that she is our Mother and "never was it known that anyone who fled to her protection or sought her aid was left unaided."

Our Solitary Boast

"Rejoice, O highly favored daughter."

Luke 1:28

One of the most awesome attributes of God is his humility. Our loving Father graciously condescends to accommodate himself to our physical, psychological, intellectual and spiritual limitations. Because of his profound humility, God also has a sense of humor.

God manifested this sense of humor with respect to his own Mother and her relationship with us. In 1854 the Church declared Mary, the Mother of Jesus, to be the Immaculate Conception.

Certain teachers and theologians questioned this declaration and the advisability of this pronouncement at that particular time. Just four years after this solemn declaration, God permitted his Mother to appear many times to St. Bernadette Soubirous at Lourdes in France. Here Mary announced to the world through this young seer: "I am the Immaculate Conception." This chronological sequence of events certainly manifests God's wonderful sense of humor.

The Church has always believed that God preserved Mary from the slightest stain of sin from the very moment of her conception. Throughout the centuries, the Church has honored Mary as the only person who was preserved from the slightest effects of sin. This formal declaration came at this time to focus our attention once again upon Mary's unique privilege and also to encourage us to honor her for this special prerogative with which God favored her.

In his divine plan of salvation God intended to ask Mary to become the Mother of his Son, Jesus. If Mary is to fulfill this important maternal role, it is only fitting and proper that she who was to give birth to the Sinless One, should be free from all sin and its effects.

The sanctifying power of God had preserved her as the angel Gabriel implied in his greeting to Mary: "Rejoice, O highly favored daughter! The Lord is with you. Blessed are you among women" (*Luke 1:28*).

Elizabeth, too, understood the uniqueness of Mary's vocation. She did not hesitate to cry out in a loud voice: "Blest are you among women and blest is the fruit of your womb. But who am I that the mother of my Lord should come to me?" (*Luke 1:42f*).

20

Mary, too, realized what a great prerogative was hers and in her humility she understood perfectly that it was all a gift from God. She joyously hymned her praise to God in her Canticle:

"My being proclaims the greatness of the Lord,
my spirit finds joy in God my savior,
For he has looked upon his servant in her lowliness
all ages to come shall call me blessed.
God who is mighty has done great things for me,
holy is his name."

We, too, rejoice with Mary; we, too, praise God with her as we sing her Canticle each day in the prayer of the Church.

As we ponder Mary's great privilege, her Immaculate Conception, we are moved to a much greater appreciation of God's loving concern for his sinful creatures. God promised mankind a Savior who would redeem us so that we could rise and be happily united with him for all eternity.

As the time approaches, our loving Father meticulously plans and prepares Mary for her special mission in life. His presence and his power is so evident in this great event of salvation history.

God prepared Mary even before she was born by preserving her, from the moment of her conception, from all sin and its disastrous effects. When the time came, God manifested his omnipotence:

> "The Holy Spirit will come upon you and the power of the Most High will overshadow you; hence the holy offspring to be born will be called Son of God" (*Luke 1:35*).

What mercy and compassion the Father manifests to us in his provident love and concern for us his wayward children.

Mary's vocation is unique and extraordinary. However, in God's divine design he calls each one of us to a very special mission in life. That mission unfolds as life marches on. However, there is one phase which is apparent from the early years of our life.

God has called each one of us to love him in our own personal way. No one else could ever fulfill this part of our mission.

Our Father has other special plans for us. Listen to him explain his providential concern for each one of us. He says through his prophet:

> "For I know well the plans I have in mind for you, says the Lord, plans for your welfare, not for woe! plans to give you a

future full of hope . . . . *(Jeremiah 29:11ff)*.

Mary continuously died to self; hence, she could give herself unreservedly to God's will in her life. As we die to self each day, as we strive to keep ourselves from sin, we too will be able to hear God's call more easily and will more readily be able to respond as generously and graciously as Mary did.

Surely: "God who is mighty has done great things for me."

Summit Meeting

"Blest are you among women."

Luke 1:39-45

At times in our lives when we have experienced great joy, we have found that we simply cannot contain ourselves. We have to share it with someone. We may even wish to shout it from the housetops. As we shared our joy we discovered its intensity increased and brought joy to others. Likewise, if we share our sorrow or disappointment with some understanding person, our pain and sorrow diminish greatly.

We have found too that if our joy was caused by some extraordinary experience, we did not feel that we could share it with everyone. We could share it only with a person who would understand.

Joy filled Mary's heart to the breaking point when she began to comprehend more fully the import of the angel's message. God had chosen her to be the channel through which his divine Son would come into the world. Furthermore, she was to become a Mother and yet retain her virginity. Who could understand such a mysterious phenomenon? Who could believe it? Never had it occurred in the annals of human history.

Mary was compelled to share this joy which overwhelmed her. Her heart just could not contain it. Mary then remembered the sign which the angel had given her. "Know that Elizabeth your kinswoman has conceived a son in her old age; she who was thought to be sterile is now in her sixth month" (*Luke 1:36*).

When she recalled these words of the angel, "Mary set out, proceeding in haste into the hill country to a town of Judah, where she entered Zechariah's house and greeted Elizabeth" (*Luke 1:39-40*).

Some misgivings must have been in Mary's heart as she prepared to leave for Ain Karem. In the first place, Mary herself was now pregnant. Would the journey be too strenuous and too long? Should she risk it?

Furthermore, her journey to Zechariah's home would take her through alien Samaritan territory. Should she venture to travel through this unfriendly country and endanger her mission in life?

How would she, a girl from Galilee, be received by the sophisticated society of Jerusalem and its suburbs? The people of Galilee were considered backwoods people, uncultured and unlettered.

If such fears came into Mary's mind she, being a woman of prayer, quickly dispelled them. In her prayer she was always in close communion with God; always open and receptive; attuned to do his will. Mary was moved by the Holy Spirit who filled her whole being since her Immaculate Conception. What joy, what reassurance must have prompted her as she joined the caravan going south to Jerusalem.

When Mary arrived in Zechariah's house, Luke tells us Elizabeth was filled with the Holy Spirit and cried out with a loud voice: "Who am I that the mother of my Lord should come to me?" Elizabeth recognized Mary's special prerogative. The sign given her was the fact that the infant in her womb leapt with joy.

Elizabeth, like Mary, was a woman of faith. She realized that nothing is impossible with God for she was about to become a mother at an age far beyond the childbearing years.

Elizabeth, too, was open and receptive to the Holy Spirit. It was through the revelation of the Holy Spirit within her that she recognized Mary as the "mother of my Lord."

Elizabeth was loud in her praise of what God was doing in Mary. Her words can be on our lips daily when we pray with her: "Blest are you among women and blest is the fruit of your womb."

Humanly speaking, Elizabeth's reaction could

have been otherwise. For many years she lived with the humiliation of being childless in a culture which considered barrenness a sign of God's disfavor. Throughout those years she must have been persecuted frequently by her own peers.

The fact that Elizabeth's husband, Zechariah, belonged to the priestly caste must have raised many questions, and perhaps even aspersions on his priestly ministry.

What husband living in those times would not have been disappointed in not having any children to carry on the family name? This was considered a punishment from God.

However, our loving Father tells us: ". . . my thoughts are not your thoughts, nor are your ways my ways" *(Isaiah 55:8)*. After years of conditioning, God not only blessed Zechariah and Elizabeth with a child, but with a son of whom our Lord could say: "I solemnly assure you, history has not known a man born of woman greater than John the Baptizer."

Imagine the joy of that meeting between Mary and Elizabeth! These two hearts beat in unison; they understood each other and the privileged mission to which each of them was called. How their hearts rejoiced as they sang the praises of the goodness of the Lord!

Mary and Elizabeth teach us that dynamic, expectant faith helps God accomplish his purpose in us, a purpose which brings a tremendous bonus —

a peace and joy which this world cannot give!

A Humble Heart Rejoices

"My being proclaims the greatness of the Lord."

Luke 1:46-55

When we receive good news our hearts dance with joy and we easily break into song. Song is the verbalized melody of the heart echoing our interior joy.

When Mary and Elizabeth shared their mutual secrets of all the wonderful and mysterious things that God was doing in them and through them, Mary could not contain the tremendous joy which overflowed her heart. She burst into song just as we are apt to do when joy fills our hearts.

From the depth of her whole being her song of joy rang out: "My being proclaims the greatness of the Lord, my spirit finds joy in God my Savior."

Mary's canticle has become one of the greatest hymns in the Church. It has reverberated down through the ages. Daily it reechoes thousands of times throughout the world.

The Magnificat is saturated with the Old Testament. Mary recalls the words of the prophets: "Even as he promised our fathers, promised Abraham and his descendants forever." It is closely related to Hannah's song in praise of Yahweh (I Samuel 2:1-10). Hannah thanked God because she had borne a son despite her sterility. She praised God as the helper of the weak, who casts down the mighty and raises up the lowly. For Hannah, God alone is the true source of strength.

In her hymn of praise Mary does the same. In doing so she reveals the genuine humility of her heart. She rejoiced at the presence of God in her life; gave credit where credit was due; and gave all the praise to God. This is genuine humility.

Humility has been defined as the truth — the truth about God and the truth about ourselves. Jesus said: ". . . apart from me you can do nothing" (John 15:5). Mary humbly acknowledges her own lowliness and attributes all to God. Listen to her words: "God who is mighty has done great things for me, holy is his name."

Perhaps at some time we have found ourselves helpless in a given situation. Suddenly our loving Father comes to our rescue with a power far beyond our comprehension. We cannot help but stand in awe and reverence of his divine presence and power. In the face of these divine manifestations we become humble. As we contemplate

God's power in our midst, we like Mary, can sing: "God who is mighty has done great things for me."

Mary's humility is authentic. There is nothing phony about her. There is no pseudo-humility about her. A pseudo-humble person is inclined to disclaim the reality of a gift or talent. He or she tries to conceal it. Genuine humility, on the other hand, openly recognizes the gift and gives all the praise to God.

There is another kind of pseudo-humility which is often called "humility with a hook." A person may try to deny or belittle a gift or talent, maintaining that he or she does not really possess such a gift, or at least not to any eminent degree. That person does so with a purpose, harboring the hope that the other person will reassure them and reaffirm their giftedness. They are in reality reaching out for a compliment.

Certainly Mary's humility was in no way a pseudo-humility — hers was genuine. Mary was a young girl fresh from the hill country of Galilee with little or no formal education or social standing according to worldly standards. She arrived in the midst of an affluent and cultured society. Her own kin belonged to the priestly caste. All this did not influence Mary in the slightest. She was radiant with joy. Humbly and confidently she sang: "For he has looked upon his servant in her lowliness; all ages to come shall call me blessed."

Mary did not hesitate to proclaim the fact that she was chosen by God for an extraordinary mission in life. Nor did she hesitate to say: "All ages to come shall call me blessed." She could do so without a blush because in her humility she immediately adds: "God who is mighty has done great things for me." Mary recognized and proclaimed the handiwork of God and attributed nothing to herself.

We too are chosen by God. Our loving Father has a special and specific mission for each one of us. Our mission in life is important to God. If we fail him, no one else can take our place. God has created us to love him. No one else can do that for us.

If we love God we can accept graciously and generously whatever plans our Father has for us. It requires humility to give our unconditional yes to the Father. In the *Spiritual Exercises,* St. Ignatius defines the first kind of humility as humbling ourselves to obey the law of God our Lord in all things. This kind is necessary for salvation.

Jesus taught us the importance of humility when he said: "I assure you, unless you change and become like little children, you will not enter the kingdom of God. Whoever makes himself lowly, becoming like this child, is of greatest importance in that heavenly reign" *(Matthew 18:3f)*.

Jesus also warned us: "Whoever exalts himself shall be humbled, but whoever humbles himself shall be exalted" *(Matthew 23:12)*.

Furthermore Jesus teaches us genuine humility by his own example and bids us: ". . . learn from me, for I am gentle and humble of heart" *(Matthew 11:29)*.

A Joyous Heart Sings

Luke 1:46-55

One of the special blessings from our loving Father in heaven is genuine Christian joy. He wants us to be a happy, joyous people.

Our Blessed Mother was a person filled with joy, one who had reason to be a happy, joyous person. Her canticle reflects this joy which filled her heart.

After centuries of waiting for the coming of the Messiah, God was now fulfilling the promises he had made to his people throughout the centuries, promises reiterated by prophets in every age. What joy the knowledge of this fulfillment must have brought to Mary and to all those who were involved in the secret of God's salvific action in their lives!

Mary was joyous because her people were now to be saved and brought to their eternal union with God. Mary was the first to know that "God so loved the world that he gave his only

Son, that whoever believes in him may not die but have eternal life" *(John 3:16)*

Even before the dawn of the Christian era, the theme of hope and joy was woven throughout the fabric of the Old Testament. How often the psalmist's heart was overwhelmed with joy as he reflected on the goodness and love of God for each one of us.

Listen to the joy radiating through the psalmist's prayer: "You will show me the path of life, fullness of joys in your presence, the delights at your right hand forever" *(Psalm 16:11)*. The psalmist recognizes that only God can give genuine, interior joy: "You put gladness into my heart, more than when grain and wine abound," *(Psalm 4:8)* and invites us to rejoice with him when he reminds us: "This is the day the Lord has made; let us be glad and rejoice in it" *(Psalm 118:24)*.

The coming of Jesus into the world was certainly reason for great joy. When the angel appeared to the shepherds in the fields near Bethlehem, he said: ". . . I come to proclaim good news to you — tidings of great joy to be shared by the whole people" *(Luke 2:10)*.

Our loving Father wants us to be a joyous people. Here again Mary is the model for our emulation. Perhaps no other human being ever suffered as much as she did, yet few if any experienced greater joy than she did.

35

Jesus taught us that suffering and pain are not incompatible with joy. "I tell you truly, you will weep and mourn while the world rejoices; you will grieve for a time, but your grief will be turned to joy" (John 16:20).

The chosen people of old experienced suffering, but found peace and joy as the psalmist relates: "Those that sow in tears shall reap rejoicing. Although they go forth weeping, carrying the seed to be sown, they shall come back rejoicing, carrying their sheaves" (Psalm 126:5f)

Mary knew the pain of suffering, but her sinlessness enabled her to end the misery and unhappiness which would come to her people because they rejected Jesus as the Messiah. Soothing this pain and raising her above it was also Mary's knowledge of the Father's infinite love for each one of us. This was the source of Mary's joy; that was why her spirit found joy in God our Savior.

"Mary treasured all these things and reflected on them in her heart." As she spent time in this contemplation she was able to recognize God's presence, his power and his love in everything which was taking place at that stage of salvation history.

As Mary spent time alone with God in prayer, she stood in awe and reverence as she contemplated his inscrutable judgments and his unsearchable ways. This was the fountain of her great joy.

Jesus wants us to be a happy, joyous people. Did he not assure us: "All this I tell you that my joy may be yours and your joy may be complete" (John15:11)? Jesus revealed the Good News to us so we would find great peace and joy.

Jesus also revealed to us the Good News that his Father loves us, that we are his children. In doing so, Jesus reminds us that he himself loves us. How simply, but how beautifully he says: "As the Father has loved me, so I have loved you. Live on in my love" (John 15:9)

When we know that we are loved and that we are lovable, we will be happy persons. This truth also keeps us humble, realizing that God loves us just as we are with all our humaness, our faults and failures, our weakness and waywardness.

Genuine Christian joy is not a perpetual state of hilarity. By no means! True joy is the interior peace and happiness which comes from the awareness that God really does love us, combined with the knowledge that we are striving to re-spond to that love. This awareness must come from our heart. We will become more and more aware of his enduring love. Our contemplative prayer, like Mary's, is our response in love to God.

This is the kind of joy of which St. Paul speaks when he exhorts us: "Rejoice in the Lord always! I say it again. Rejoice!" (Philippians 4:4).

Love Causes Pain

"It is by the Holy Spirit
that she has conceived this child."

Matthew 1:18-25

To our western culture the phraseology of this Gospel narrative may seem a little confusing, and the relationship between Mary and Joseph a little bewildering.

According to the customs of that time, a boy and girl were engaged as mere children. The engagement was arranged by the parents before the children even knew each other.

The second stage was the betrothal. This was the ratification of the engagement made years earlier. The betrothal could be broken at this stage if one of the parties did not want to proceed with the marriage.

The betrothal lasted for at least one year during which time the couple were called husband and wife even though they did not have the rights of husband and wife. This betrothal could be terminated only by divorce. The last state in this process was the marriage proper.

Mary and Joseph had been engaged as children and had already entered into the stage of betrothal when Joseph realized Mary was pregnant.

God's salvific plan for mankind began to evolve. Joseph and Mary were from the line of David. "Jacob was the father of Joseph the husband of Mary. It was of her that Jesus who is called Messiah was born" *(Matthew 1:16).*

Mary and Joseph were called by God for a very special mission in life. It was initiated when the Angel Gabriel announced to Mary: "You shall conceive and bear a son and give him the name Jesus" *(Luke 1:31).* Exuberant with joy, Mary set out, proceeding in haste into the hill country to a town of Judah where she entered Zechariah's house and greeted Elizabeth. "Mary remained with Elizabeth about three months and then returned home" *(Luke 1:56).*

When Joseph discovered that Mary was with child, a dark cloud descended to dampen and almost obliterate their beautiful love relationship. We can well imagine the sinister shadow of doubt robbing Joseph of the peace and joy for which his heart longed. He wanted to believe, to trust Mary implicitly, but the concrete evidence was too convincing for him.

Joseph loved Mary dearly. He did not want to

cause her pain, yet according to the custom of his day he could not accept her into his household. He could not bear to expose her. He pondered his next action with a leaden heart.

Mary's anguish was no less intense. She loved Joseph and this caused the pain of being under suspicion to be even more severe. There was no way in which she could have explained to Joseph what was happening. Never before in the annals of human history had such an event taken place. It was beyond the ability of finite minds to comprehend.

When God calls us to a special mission, we must be conditioned to accept and fulfill our apostolate. Mary and Joseph had to mature in their trust of God and their trust in each other. This was a period of probation and testing for them. According to God's plan they would have to face some impossible situations in the years to come.

How frequently God must remind us: "For my thoughts are not your thoughts, nor are your ways my ways" (Isaiah 55:8). Since we cannot comprehend God's designs, he asks us to trust him.

Emerging from this crisis situation, Mary is again the marvelous exemplar. She teaches us so many virtues.

In the first place, Mary's patience was very pronounced. How patiently she waited for the

Lord's plan to evolve! She waited not so much to be vindicated, but to permit God's plan to unfold for his greater honor and glory.

We cannot help but be moved by Mary's silence and humility. She did not try to defend herself. She did not cry out against the injustice of the suspicions which she must have felt. She remained silent, confident that God's purpose would eventually be effected.

Mary exemplified total trust and confidence in God even in the midst of this turmoil. It is easy to trust a person when all is going well, but when strife and difficulties arise many doubts and fears clamor for a place in our mind.

When the angel asked Mary to become the Mother of the Messiah, Mary did not hesitate even though such a thing had never occurred before. Mary asked only one question to clarify exactly how God's will was to be accomplished in her life. What a noble example of trust in God's loving care!

All these virtues were possible because Mary loved. Her love for God was tremendous. Love trusts implicitly, regardless of the circumstances.

How encouragingly St. John expresses it: "Love has no room for fear; rather, perfect love casts out all fear" (I John 4:18).

The secret of Mary's trust, her patient endurance, her silent humility is her love.

Jesus invites us: "Live on in my love" (John 15:9).

41

Prayer is the Key

"Mary treasured all these things
and reflected on them in her heart."

Luke 2:8-20

Mary is our model in prayer. Mary lived prayerfully. Mary lived contemplatively. One of the dimensions of Mary's prayer life is revealed to us at Bethlehem.

The shepherds came with haste and repeated to Mary and Joseph what the angels had told them: "I come to proclaim good news to you — tidings of great joy to be shared by the whole people. This day in David's city a savior has been born to you, the Messiah and Lord" (*Luke 2:10f*).

In this one brief statement the unfathomable mystery of God's redeeming love is revealed. This "infant wrapped in swaddling clothes" is the "Savior" of mankind. Even though he is at the moment a helpless child, totally dependent upon others, he will save his people. What a challenge to faith!

He is also the "Messiah." This infant is the "Anointed One" of God. He is the one who has been promised down through the ages. He will deliver his people even though he lies here help-less. This truth at the moment is a difficult one for the human mind to grasp, yet faith predominates.

He is likewise "Lord." Hidden beneath the weakness of a child is the Lord of the entire universe, the Creator of the sun, moon and stars. His guiding hand holds in balance all of creation. How can finite minds comprehend the immensity of this mystery?

Mary holds the key which unlocks the secret. God had prepared Mary for this great mystery. Her humility, her reverence, her total orientation of self to God were attitudes which she had ac-quired through long hours of prayer before she was touched by God. Mary was a person of great faith.

Faith does not come easily. Did Mary not question the angel: "How can this be since I do not know man?" (Luke 1:34). How could she believe without hesitation and doubt?

Her secret was prayer. In her prayer Mary was transformed by God. The Holy Spirit found her truly pliable and receptive to his mysterious workings within her.

Her response to this marvelous operation of God in her life was to reflect, to ponder, to con-template. "Mary treasured all these things and reflected on them in her heart."

She had been formed by the silent, dynamic presence of God within her. Her prayer kept her in tune with the powerful workings of God. Her prayer enriched her with a new depth of wisdom. In her wisdom she asked no questions. She reflected. This was Mary's habitual response to mystery: silent, prayerful reflection.

Mary's life of prayer led her to a total absorption in God present to her and dwelling within her. Even though the mystery remained unfathomable, Mary gladly and joyfully accepted whatever role God wanted her to fulfill. Her peace and joy radiated throughout her whole being.

Prayer united her very closely and very intimately with God. Her heart beat in unison with his. All this was the fruit of her life of prayer.

Mary's prayerful and reverent attitude also touched the shepherds. St. Luke tells us that the shepherds went with haste and "once they saw, they understood." How much Mary's attitude helped them to understand we will never know. Surely her faith, her joy, her prayer must have had its influence on them.

What a transformation took place within them! "The shepherds returned, glorifying and praising God for all they had heard and seen."

Mary fulfilled the role to which she was called to perfection. She was able to do so because she was formed and transformed by prayer. Mary's life is not impossible for us. The Second Vatican Council assures us that Mary heard the word of God and kept it. Thus she has become a model for all the members of the Church. As we come to listen like Mary did, then our life, our love, our union with Jesus - Savior - Messiah - Lord will be perfected.

Mary is our model in prayer because she is the listener par excellence.

Sign of Contradiction

"You yourself shall be pierced with a sword."

Luke 2:22-40

Mary is rightly called the Queen of Martyrs. While she did not suffer physical martyrdom, her sufferings were so intense that it was tantamount to a spiritual martyrdom. Because of her sinlessness Mary felt more keenly the rejection shown to her Son; too, she saw her own people turning away from the long promised joy of salvation.

In Israel, at that time, there were many awaiting some kind of celestial champion, a descendent of David who would make the chosen people masters of the world and lords of all the nations. They believed God would break directly into history and effect this domination by supernatural means.

On the other hand there were many who, like Joseph and Mary, Simeon and Anna, were patiently and prayerfully waiting for a Messiah, a Savior, who would restore joy and peace to the

hearts of men through a more personal relationship with God. These people recognized the fet-
ters of sin which alienated them from their loving
Father.

How Mary's heart must have rejoiced as she
prayed with Zechariah: "Blessed be the Lord the
God of Israel because he has visited and ransomed
his people" *(Luke 1:68)*. The joy overflowing her
heart was marred by the sword of sorrow which
Simeon predicted.

Listen with Mary as Simeon says: "This child
is destined to be the downfall . . . of many in
Israel." This was a strange and hard saying about
the One who had come to save his people; however, it becomes clearer when we realize that
Jesus came to bring the Good News of salvation
to all people. There were many who would respond in joy and humility and who would embrace the new way with faith and love; on the
other hand there would be many who would re-
main unmoved or even actively hostile, refusing
to accept the Good News. God does not judge
people; rather, each person judges himself or
herself by accepting or refusing Jesus.

Mary felt this pain of rejection as a piercing
sword in her heart: her own people turning away
from the peace and joy of salvation by rejecting
her Son and the Father's plan for them. She could
have anticipated her Son's words: "Father, forgive them; they do not know what they are

doing" *(Luke 23:34)*.

"This child is destined to be . . . the rise of many in Israel." Through his death and resurrection Jesus conquered sin and Satan. Jesus would be the "rise" for many in Israel and throughout the world in the ages to come. Mary's heart rejoiced at this prospect, but again the stabbing sword of rejection pierced her as she realized how many would refuse to accept the love and divine life which Jesus was so eager to share with them.

"A sign that will be opposed:" Jesus and his message of love would be joyfully and fruitfully accepted by some, but also bitterly opposed by many. There is no room for neutrality here. Jesus said very clearly: "He who is not with me is against me, and he who does not gather with me scatters" *(Luke 11:23)*.

If we do not surrender to Jesus then we are at war with him. It is so tragic that pride keeps many from surrendering to Jesus. Surrender leads to peace, life, victory!

Mary was a delicately thoughtful person because she was not scarred by the effects of sin. She comprehended this profound mystery of salvation and the infinite love which it embodied; hence the pain which rejection must have brought to her.

Mary was closely linked with Jesus in his sorrowful, redemptive work. Each rejection was another sword piercing her Immaculate Heart. She loved her own people. She knew the longing

48

of their hearts. As she witnessed their rejection of her Son, she experienced untold pain.

It is not our intention to dwell on the sword of suffering which pierced Mary's heart in order to experience the pain with her. Rather, our contemplation of her suffering will help us to appreciate more and more the gift of our own faith.

It should move us into a deeper spirit of gratitude to our loving, gracious Father who loved us so much that he gave us his own Divine Son. Mary's example of willing acceptance of her role and her unconditional 'fiat' will encourage us to say yes to the Father.

Simeon and Anna mapped out the way for us. Their long hours, days and years spent in prayer enabled them to penetrate the mystery of Jesus hidden under the cloak of his frail humanity.

In prayer the Holy Spirit will reveal to us the mystery of God's love for us, enabling us, like Mary, to respond graciously and generously to his love without counting the pain which is often a part of it.

Escape to Egypt

"Get up, take the child and his mother,
and flee to Egypt."

Matthew 2:13-18

God implanted in our human nature a desire to love and to be loved. When we are accepted by others we have the assurance that we are lovable. The desire for acceptance is so great that any sort of rejection causes us much pain.

Even a cursory survey of the Gospels discloses numerous times Jesus was rejected. In fact, his whole public ministry is one long series of rejections.

One of the first rejections came soon after his birth. He was still a helpless child when Herod learned of his birth. Herod's insane fear of being deposed or of being supplanted by another king drove him to a cruel, murderous attack on all innocent male children under two years of age. He hoped that Jesus would be among them.

God had other plans even though there was

much pain involved. To avoid Herod's insidious plot "the angel of the Lord suddenly appeared in a dream to Joseph with the command: 'Get up, take the child and his mother, and flee to Egypt. Stay there until I tell you otherwise. Herod is searching for the child to destroy him.' "

Rejection is a severe pain which pierces the heart and permeates one's whole being. Mary experienced every pang of rejection directed toward her Son.

At the very beginning of his life God's Son was rejected. Even though he brought the divine gift of salvation to the world, he had to be eliminated. Herod would be satisfied with nothing less than his death. Even though he was too young to utter a word in his own defense, he had to be destroyed. Mary understood, yet the pain penetrated deeply into her heart.

"Yes, God so loved the world that he gave his only Son, that whoever believes in him may not die but may have eternal life" *(John 3:16)*. Even though God was willing to give us his only Son, human beings decreed that if that Son would interfere with their plans or if his life was in any way a rebuke to their ambitions, then he must be eliminated at any price. That was the rejection which Mary understood so keenly.

How dreadfully accurate was Simeon's prophecy: "You yourself shall be pierced with a sword." The sword of rejection is sharp, two-edged, penetrating.

There is another sorrow which Mary suffered which only a mother can understand. A mother loves her child and is proud of her offspring. She wants to live close to those near and dear to her and to share her joy at the miracle of a new life! Mary was deprived of that joy and consolation. Instead, she had to flee to a strange land, a foreign country.

There was little consolation awaiting Mary and Joseph in Egypt. Whenever any strife broke out in Israel, some of the Jews escaped to Egypt. In almost every little village or town there were some pockets of her own people. Even so, it was a foreign land, far from family and friends. Separation from home is even more painful in times of trouble. We naturally want to be close to those we love when we are suffering. This too added to the intensity of Mary's suffering.

Even though Mary's pain was severe, she still trusted God. Somehow all this fit into God's plans even though she could not understand it. She had given her unconditional 'fiat' and she would never renege on that. She must have found consolation in the words of Jeremiah: "For I know well the plans I have in mind for you . . . plans for your welfare, not for woe! plans to give you a future full of hope" (*Jeremiah 29:11*).

Today the rejection of Jesus continues. If Jesus and his way of life seem to interfere with peoples' plans and ambitions, if his moral code rebukes their own conduct, then Jesus and his teachings must be eliminated. Thus the rejection goes on even though Jesus continues to reach out in love.

How often I have rejected Jesus! Perhaps I hesitate to come to know him better because he may ask too much. How often my time alone with him in prayer has been abbreviated or skipped altogether because other lesser priorities demanded my time and attention. In my value system I had more important things to do!

"Come, Lord Jesus, free me from the exile of Egypt to which I have been banished by you. Come, walk with me, work with me, wander with me as I endeavor to find you in all things."

A Painful Search

"I have been searching for you in sorrow."

Luke 2:41-52

The annual pilgrimage to the Holy City for the feast of the Passover was a joyous occasion for Mary and Joseph. Each year they looked forward with great anticipation to this spiritually uplifting celebration. How they must have looked forward to Jesus' twelfth birthday when he would accompany them to the Temple. Little did they realize what sorrow it would temporarily bring them.

The loss of Jesus was understandable. There were no superhighways, no rapid transit systems, no trains or buses to transport families. Travel on foot was the common means, with a beast of burden, a donkey or a camel, for the elderly or infirm. People traveled in family groups, alone or with inhabitants from the same village. Men often traveled alone in groups; so did the women, and the children frequently commuted between the two groups.

This helps us understand the scripture: "Thinking he was in the party, they continued their journey for a day, looking for him among their relatives and acquaintances."

Then the dreadful realization settled upon Mary and Joseph. Jesus was lost! They were already a full day's journey from Jersusalem. It would take another day just to return to Jerusalem. What could have happened to him in the meantime? Where could they begin to search for him?

What thoughts must have flashed through Mary's mind! Would she ever see her Son again? Did some harm befall him? Herod's attempt on his life as a small infant was still fresh in her mind. Was he already beginning his redemptive work? Would he ever return to Nazareth?

Did Mary remonstrate with herself at her carelessness in looking after her Son? Countless must have been the thoughts flashing through her mind as she and Joseph wearily trudged their way back to the Holy City. How different than a few days ago when they were eagerly and joyously chanting the psalms, as they were accustomed to do, as they approached the city. There were no bursts of joy as the golden dome of the temple came into view.

After searching for Jesus for three days, they found him in his Father's house. "On the third day they came upon him in the temple sitting in the midst of the teachers, listening to them and asking them questions."

During the Passover season it was customary for the Sanhedrin to meet in public in the Temple court to discuss religious and theological questions in the presence of all who would listen. We must not imagine that Jesus was a precocious boy lecturing to a group of Jewish leaders. "Listening to them and asking them questions" was the accepted method for a student to learn from his teachers. Jesus was listening to the discussions, searching for knowledge like a good student.

Another stab of pain must have rent Mary's heart when Jesus asked her: "Why did you search for me? Did you not know I had to be in my Father's house?" Mary was not saddened by his words, but by the realization that he had come to evangelize the entire world by proclaiming the Good News and that she would soon have to give him up.

According to the Father's decree, Jesus had to leave the peaceful confines of his home in Nazareth to begin his mission. His heart must have ached at the prospect of leaving his Mother whom he loved so dearly.

Jesus knows the pain of separation, especially that final separation caused by death. He not only said to the widow of Naim who had lost her only son, "Do not cry," but "he gave him back to his mother" (Luke 7:13ff). He spared Jairus and his wife the pain of separation when he restored their twelve-year-old daughter to them. How happy were Mary and Martha when Jesus brought Lazarus back into their household!

We too can lose Jesus. Sin is a refusal to love. Sin can separate us from the very source of divine life. By our own volition, we can sever ourselves like a branch cut off from the vine. If we have the misfortune to do so, we will experience the pain of loss.

Our own self-centeredness, our own indifference to his love will cause us to lose that peace and joy which he alone can give. Through our own lack of loving response to him, we can lose the awareness of his presence, the awareness of his love.

Mary continued to live in his presence through her long hours of prayer. Through her powerful intercession, may we never know the pain of that loss.

An Expectant Faith

"They have no more wine."

John 2:1-12

There is one special attribute with which every good mother is endowed by God. This gift is her maternal solicitude not only for her own children, but also a loving concern which reaches out to others, especially to all in need. Years of generous giving of themselves in caring for their children and others seems to make mothers more alert and more aware of others' needs. True as it is that God has gifted mothers in general with this unselfish quality, the individual mother must be open to receive this gift and cooperate generously with it in order to enhance and beautify it.

If every mother is blessed by God with this gift of gracious solicitude for others, how much more should we expect to find it in Mary, whose loving concern was not dulled by any effects of sin. At the wedding feast in Cana of Galilee, Mary manifested this maternal solicitude to an eminent degree. A wedding feast without wine was unthinkable in the days of Jesus. The rabbis said: "Without wine there is no joy." The wedding ceremony took place in the evening. After the ceremony and well-wishing, the young couple were conducted to their new home. The newly married couple did not take a honeymoon. They stayed at home and kept an open house for guests for a whole week. During this week they dressed in their wedding robes and wore crowns. We can imagine how freely the wine flowed.

Apparently Mary was the first one to notice at the Cana wedding, that the wine was running short. Instinctively she turned to her Son to apprise him of the situation. Imagine her pleading eyes as she said very simply: "They have no more wine."

Mary was probably aware that her Son's "hour" had not yet come, nevertheless that did not deter her from placing this petition before him.

The response of Jesus to his Mother's request may startle us momentarily. "Woman, how does this concern of yours involve me?" These words of Jesus were a conversational phrase commonly used at the time. Likewise, the term "Woman" cannot be translated into English. We do not have a word which expresses its exact meaning. Perhaps the word "Lady" comes closest to it. The word "woman" was by no means discourteous.

Jesus was probably saying something like this: "Don't worry, Mother; you don't quite understand what is going on; leave things to me and I will take care of them in my own way."

Jesus was fully aware of what "this first of his signs" would mean. In the first place it would bring glory to God. Secondly, it would reveal his identity so that "his disciples believed in him." Thirdly, this miracle would bring joy to the bride and groom as well as happiness to the jubilant wedding guests.

There was still another effect of this "sign." This manifestation of his divine power would enrage his enemies. He was too much for them. This sign would single out those who were for him and those who were against him. In fact, this "first of his signs" was tantamount to signing his death warrant.

In spite of all this, Jesus could hear his Mother's simple, confident plea: "They have no more wine." Mary presented this predicament to her Son with a vibrant, expectant faith. She knew her Son. He had lived with her at Nazareth for thirty years. She turned to him instinctively for help. What deep faith she manifested in him! Her faith convinced her that he would do something to relieve the embarrassment of the young bride and groom.

There are several different levels of faith. One

level of faith helps us to accept a truth even though we cannot understand or grasp it with our finite minds. This level of faith helps us give intellectual assent even though we cannot penetrate the mystery involved.

Another level of faith is even greater. When our faith in some truth or cause is so strong that we are willing to devote our time and talent to that cause, or even devote our lives to it, we have a faith of commitment.

A third level of faith is a faith of expectancy. We believe so deeply in the power and loving concern of God that we know that he will act in a given situation.

This expectant faith filled Mary's heart. She understood the heart of her Son. She knew that he would be deeply moved for the bride and groom and that he would do something to relieve the humiliation which the newly married couple would suffer.

Mary's expectant faith was so strong that she confidently instructed the waiters: "Do whatever he tells you."

How generously Jesus rewarded the faith of his Mother! In doing so, Jesus assured us that if we believe in him and trust him, our faith too will be rewarded far beyond our expectations.

Recall the occasion when the disciples could not expel the demon from a possessed boy. When Jesus appeared they appealed to him. His response was direct: "Everything is possible to a man who trusts. The boy's father immediately exclaimed, 'I do believe! Help my lack of trust' " (*Mark* 9:23f). On another occasion Jesus said: "Fear is useless. What is needed is trust" (*Mark* 5:36).

Mary's faith buoyed her up many times when God's will seemed difficult. She was able to accept the poverty of Bethlehem, the harshness of Egypt, the cruelty of Calvary because she believed in God's inscrutable plans. She trusted. She had faith.

An Extravagant Response

"Do whatever he tells you."

John 2:1-12

Early in life most of us learned about the intercessory power of our mother. Even as children we were aware of her loving concern and sensitivity. Very early in life we learned that her influence as an advocate before our father was powerful. How often as children did we not bring our desires before our mother and beg her to intercede for us with our father.

This is in no way disparaging to fathers who because of their duties outside the home are not always aware of their children's needs or desires. Often a mother is more in tune with them. In his goodness, God endowed mothers and fathers with special but very different gifts. As parents they complement each other.

Mary is our Mother. How aptly she fulfilled the role of intercessor at the wedding feast in Cana of Galilee. Her maternal solicitude enabled her to notice immediately the deficiency of wine. What a humiliation it would be to the bride and groom and what a disappointment to the guests if the supply of wine should be depleted!

Mary promptly informed Jesus of the impending embarrassment. In reply she received an apparent excuse for not being able to relieve the situation: "My hour has not yet come."

At the very outset of his public life, Jesus wanted to show us how powerful the intercession of his Mother was. Even though his "hour" had not yet come, he worked "this first of his signs" at her request. Jesus was pleased that his Mother was so concerned about the welfare of others. Note that Mary was not asking anything for herself. She was deeply concerned about the young couple and their guests.

Jesus showed his approval of his Mother's intercessory power. He responded to her petition by bidding the waiters: "Fill those water jars with water." There is another lesson contained in this request of Jesus. He could very easily have provided the water by his divine power. Jesus asks for our cooperation. The waiters' response to Jesus showed their spirit of cooperation and also their trust in him. Jesus deals with us as he did with the waiters; he asks for our cooperation and then works his wonders through us.

Jesus responded to his Mother's intercession by changing water into the best wine of the whole feast. Jesus taught us a twofold lesson. He wanted us to recognize the powerful intercession of his Mother; and he wanted to encourage us to ask her often to pray with us and for us.

The Church has always pointed to Mary's powerful intercession, both in its private as well as in its liturgical prayer. At each eucharistic celebration we honor Mary by asking her to pray for us. She is the Mother of the Church. In a unique way she is our Mother also. Her loving concern for each one of us and all our needs is just as great as it was at Cana.

As Mary prays with us she bids us, as she did the waiters at the wedding in Cana: "Do whatever he tells you." As we cheerfully accept God's will, he will supply all our needs, even those of which we are not aware.

Jesus taught us how important intercessory prayer is by his own example during his public life. He encouraged us to ask for whatever we feel we need. He expounded on the power of intercession in his Sermon on the Mount. "Ask, and you will receive. Seek, and you will find. Knock, and it will be opened to you" (Matthew 7:7). He also promised: "All you ask the Father in my name he will give you" (John 15:16).

Jesus selected three apostles to be his intercessory prayer-team. He took them with him when he raised the daughter of Jairus to life. "Once he arrived at the house, he permitted no one to enter with him except Peter, John, James, and the child's parents" *(Luke 8:51)*. On another occasion when they went up Mount Tabor to pray: "He took Peter, John and James, and went up onto a mountain to pray" *(Luke 9:28)*. It was while they were praying that Jesus was transfigured before them.

In that dreadful hour when he suffered his agony in the Garden, Jesus wanted his prayer-team close to him. "Then Jesus went with them to a place called Gethsemane. He said to his disciples, 'Stay here while I go over there and pray.' He took along Peter and Zebedee's two sons, and began to experience sorrow and distress" *(Matthew 26:36f)*.

When we intercede, it convinces us of our own poverty and our utter dependence upon God. It also helps us to clarify our needs in our own minds and helps us to make our petition more specific.

In her poverty, Mary turned to her Son for help. How those words of loving concern coming from the lips of his Mother must have touched the heart of Jesus! "They have no more wine." When we recognize our helplessness and turn to Jesus, we can be assured that he will change the mediocrity of our routine duties into the sparkling wine of loving service. All we need to do is to ask for that grace through the powerful intercession of our Mother, Mary.

"Holy Mary, Mother of God, pray for us sinners now and at the hour of our death."

Word Power

"Blest are they who hear
the word of God and keep it."

Luke 11:27-28

Mary is not only a Mother to us, but our exemplar in many ways. Jesus proudly points out to us her way of life as an exemplary means to lead us to holiness, which is the only genuine source of happiness.

One day Jesus was teaching with authority, unlike the rabbis who gave no definitive answers. When the rabbis were asked to clarify some question of law or doctrine, they merely quoted the views of other rabbis, leaving their hearers in doubt and uncertainty. On this occasion, as on others, Jesus was stating the Good News without equivocation. Furthermore, he was manifesting his divine power and his loving concern by healing and driving out evil spirits, thus bringing peace and joy to many hearts.

A certain woman in the crowd was so overwhelmed by his words and his power that she cried out a compliment in true, semitic style: "Blest is the womb that bore you and the breasts that nursed you."

Jesus must have been pleased with this compliment since it was also directed toward his Mother. As he smiled, graciously he went on to point out the real reason for his Mother's greatness. "Rather blest are they who hear the Word of God and keep it."

Mary did hear the Word of God and she did keep it. It became the guiding norm of her life. This was the real source of her holiness.

Mary understood God's Word as his personal message to her. His Word found a home in her heart. Listening long and lovingly to God's Word in prayer enabled Mary to keep her mind and heart in tune with God's will.

The Word of God has power to inspire, to convert, to transform. "God's Word is living and effective" (*Hebrews 4:12*). In God's Word we find the inspiration and motivation we need to accept cheerfully the duties of each day which can become very routine and monotonous. Only in his Word can we find that rich source of inspiration, not only to recognize God's divine plan in our daily round of duties, but to obtain the motivation to fulfill that plan to the letter.

Mary pondered God's Word as she prayed the Psalms or reflected on other parts of the Hebrew

Testament. Her prayer enabled her to discern what God wanted her to do in her special apostolate. Mary did not do anything extraordinary, but she did do all things in an extraordinary way. This is the real source of her holiness.

God's Word also has the power to condition us. ". . . it judges the reflections and thought of the heart" (*Hebrews 4:12*). Mary was not scarred by even the slightest sin. She saw easily and accepted willingly God's divine designs in her life.

We are not so fortunate. We are wounded and blinded by sin which makes us self-centered, proud, determined to do our own will. There is much need for conversion in our lives.

As we expose our thinking to his Word in prayer, a conversion begins to take place within us even though we may not be aware of it. As we permit his Word to dwell in our hearts, a change takes place within us. This conversion process is one of the many blessings wrought by his Word. Often the conversion is painless. Frequently, it takes place without our being aware of any change.

Likewise, the Word of the Lord transforms us. As we pray with his Word, as we reflect on the humility, the meekness, the sensitivity, the loving concern of Jesus as portrayed in his Word, a transformation is wrought within us. Our mentality, our thoughts, our attitudes are gradually transformed according to the mind and heart of

Jesus. St. Paul explains the fruit of praying with Sacred Scripture in these words: "All of us, gazing on the Lord's glory with unveiled faces, are being transformed from glory to glory into his very image by the Lord who is the Spirit" (*II Corinthians 3:18*).

As we pray with his Word, we become more and more singleminded with our vision ever fixed on Jesus. If our focus is riveted on Jesus, it will affect all our thoughts, words and actions. This transformation helps us adjust our priorities.

In the Gospel scene Jesus is telling us that his Mother's real holiness lies in the fact that she did hear the Word of God and that she did keep it. Jesus explained that even the honor of being his Mother could not compare with the greatness which she attained by pondering and keeping his Word.

In this account Jesus was explaining to his hearers and to us that those who come to him merely to see some sort of epiphany or to witness some miracle would not achieve holiness.

Did he not say previously: "None of those who cry out, 'Lord, Lord,' will enter the kingdom of God but only the one who does the will of my Father in heaven" (*Matthew 7:21*).

After Jesus had fed the multitude with "five barley loaves and a couple of dried fish" the crowd sought him out the next day. When they found him Jesus admonished them: "I assure you,

you are not looking for me because you have seen signs but because you have eaten your fill of the loaves. You should not be working for perishable food but for food that remains unto life eternal" (*John 6:26f*).

Mary is the supreme example of a receptive hearer. That is why she is "blest."

His Devoted Disciple

"Whoever does the will of my heavenly Father
is brother and sister and mother to me."

Matthew 12:46-50

We readily think of Mary as the Mother of
Jesus and our Mother, too. Mary is a Mother in
every sense of the term. She fulfills another important role in the economy of salvation.

Mary is a disciple of Jesus. A disciple is one
who is called by God to fulfill a special role in his
divine plan. Mary was called and prepared by
God from all eternity for her special mission.

In its Liturgy the Church applies these words
of St. Paul to Mary: "Those he predestined he
likewise called; those he called he justified; and
those he justified he in turn glorified" (*Romans
8:28-30*). These words are aptly applied to Mary
and the special role to which she was called.

Mary's call to discipleship became unmis-
takably clear when the Angel Gabriel appeared to
her and asked her to become the Mother of the

Messiah. There could not have been any mistaking the call of the Lord. It came as a personal invitation.

This incident was also the beginning of Mary's total commitment to discipleship. Can there be any doubt about the totality of her commitment when she responded: "I am the servant of the Lord. Let it be done to me as you say" (Luke 1:26-38).

During the days of his public ministry Jesus directed our focus on the real role of Mary and how graciously and faithfully she fulfilled her mission.

On one occasion Jesus took the opportunity to point out Mary's role as a disciple. One day as he was addressing the crowd, they told him that his Mother and brothers and sisters were asking for him and wanted to speak to him.

The evangelist tells us that Jesus extended his hand toward his disciples and said: "There are my mother and my brothers. Whoever does the will of my Heavenly Father is brother and sister and mother to me" (Matthew 12:46-50).

There is no offense to his Mother in these words of Jesus. He was not ignoring her. He was trying to tell us that Mary's spiritual relationship to him was far more important than her human relationship. Again Jesus was explaining that Mary's role as his disciple was more important than her role as his Mother. God could have chosen any woman. Mary's response of loving fidelity was the cause of her real greatness.

Mary was able to become a disciple of Jesus, able to fulfill the many other roles to which she was called because of her life of union with the Father, her closeness with Jesus, and her receptivity to the Holy Spirit operative within her. This was her life of prayer.

During her early years Mary must have been receptive and pliable to the formation of the Holy Spirit within her for she was sinless. Her sinlessness removed every obstacle to the influence of grace.

Likewise, her years at Nazareth were also a time of contemplative prayer. Nazareth was a house of prayer. How she pondered the mysterious workings of God in her life!

Jesus invites us to ponder prayerfully, as Mary did, our own call to discipleship. When the two disciples of John the Baptist followed Jesus as he left the River Jordan, he turned to them and asked: "What are you looking for?" It was then that Jesus invited them to "Come and see" (*John 1:35ff*). Jesus was not inviting them to come to see the type of dwelling in which he was staying. No, he was inviting them to come to stay with him to discover who he was, what he stood for, what his teaching was, what his mentality was.

A disciple is more than a student who merely listens to the master's lecture. A disciple practically lives with his master, learning by observation. He strives to captivate the mentality, the attitudes, the feelings, the heart of the master. He observes the master as he relates to the many and varied situations of everyday living.

Jesus called his followers to this same type of training. He wanted them with him, to follow him, to listen to him, to become one mind and heart with him. That is the meaning of his invitation: "Come and see." He was calling them not only to follow him but to become his disciples.

Jesus invites us to follow him so closely that we can be identified with him. St. Paul reiterates this invitation when he encourages us to "acquire a fresh, spiritual way of thinking. You must put on that new man created in God's image" *(Ephesians 4:23f)*. Again he admonishes us: "Your attitude must be that of Christ," and then proceeds to tell us what the mind of Jesus is *(Philippians 2:5ff)*.

During those thirty precious years in Nazareth, Mary was formed into a perfect disciple not only by her proximity to Jesus, but by her prayerful openness to the transforming power of the Holy Spirit.

The secret to discipleship is love. The willingness to deny oneself, to take up one's cross daily, to die to self like the grain of wheat, to eagerly give all without counting the cost, all are rooted in this love. Mary loved with an overflowing love. She loved so much she could not refrain from giving herself without reservation. Like her Son she gave herself totally to God's plan. With Jesus she prayed: "Father . . . not my will but yours be done" *(Luke 22:42)*.

An Anguished, Joyful Encounter

"Come, all you who pass by the way,
look and see whether there is any suffering
like my suffering."

Lamentations 1:12

How vividly Isaiah foretold this painful encounter which took place along the sorrowful way of the cross when Jesus came face to face with his Mother. The prophet described Jesus in these pitiable terms:

"He was spurned and avoided by men,
    a man of suffering, accustomed to
        infirmity,
One of those from whom men hide their
    faces,
    spurned, and we held him in no
        esteem" (Isaiah 53:3).

This is the person Mary met on that first Good Friday. This is her Son. He is also the Son in whom the Father is well pleased.

In our prayer we can permit our imagination to reconstruct the events which might have occurred in quick succession. Jesus fell helplessly beneath the weight of his cross. Be assured that if it were possible, his Mother would be the first to rush to his aid. It was then that Simon of Cyrene was pressed into service because Jesus was growing weaker with every step.

We do not know whether or not Jesus and his Mother exchanged words of comfort when they met. However, when two people love each other dearly heart speaks to heart more eloquently than words.

When we are suffering, it is always good to have those near and dear to us close by our side. In their presence we find great consolation, comfort and strength.

Mary's presence along the *Via Dolorosa* brought Jesus the reassurance of her undying commitment and love for him, her Son and her God. He was experiencing vicious rejection on all sides, but his Mother's loving presence overshadowed all the scorn, the ridicule, the insults and blasphemy.

How eloquently her presence spoke to Jesus about her total oblation of herself to the Father. Could any oblation be more complete than Mary's when she announced without any reservation: "I am the servant of the Lord. Let it be done to me as you say" *(Luke 1:38)*. This total gift of herself to the Father's will and her union with him in his suffering brought Jesus much peace and comfort.

There is an incomprehensible aura about suffering. It is a mystery we can never quite fathom. There is only one key which gives us a little insight into the secret of suffering. That key is love!

If we love, we must give. The degree of our giving depends upon the intensity of our love. Jesus loved with an infinite love. He could give nothing less than the total gift of himself, every last drop of his blood. Mary's love was also tremendous. She had to give herself completely without counting the cost.

Mary was conceived without any mar of sin. The fruits of the redemption were preapplied to her. She, without any inhibitions, was the perfect temple of the Holy Spirit. She was the perfect vessel to be filled with the Spirit, the source of love. St. Paul reminds us: ". . . the love of God has been poured out in our hearts through the Holy Spirit who has been given to us" *(Romans 5:5)*.

Mary experienced the infinite love which God was pouring out upon her. Because of her sinlessness, she could comprehend and experience this love to an eminent degree. Hence, she could give herself without reservation.

Jesus taught us the secret of love when he

said: "As the Father has loved me, so I have loved you. Live on in my love. You will live in my love if you keep my commandments, even as I have kept my Father's commandments, and live in his love" (John 15:9-10).

When Jesus speaks about keeping his commandments, he does not mean only the decalogue, but doing his will by preference even in the slightest matters. Love always wants to please, to give; hence, if we love a person very much, we want to fulfill his or her every desire. If this is true of human love, how much truer it is of divine love.

Mary's presence along the way to Calvary, her self-oblation in union with her Son demonstrates that she was already giving what Jesus asks us to give in each Eucharistic celebration.

When Jesus instituted the Holy Eucharist, he bade us: "Do this as a remembrance of me" (Luke 22:19). Jesus was not only requesting us to consecrate the species of bread and wine in the Eucharist; he was explaining to us that the Eucharist should also be the total gift of ourselves to the Father and climaxed in the Mass. Jesus gave his whole life to the Father from the moment he took his first breath in Bethlehem until his last agonizing breath on the cross. He gave himself completely in this climactic act of oblation.

In the Eucharist we have the same privilege of presenting ourselves and everything we do to the

Father along with Jesus who adds his own infinite dimension to our gift.

This is the great lesson which Mary teaches us along the Way of the Cross. As she gave herself with no thought of counting the cost, she encourages us to give ourselves in the same way. Furthermore, as our Mother, she is our intercessor in heaven. She is ever pleading for us that we may have the courage and generosity to dare to love to the full, and by so doing, experience a peace and joy which is not of this world.

A Mother's Fidelity

"Near the cross of Jesus there stood his Mother."

John 19:25-27

This brief statement is filled with pathos and charged with emotions. As we ponder this scene, many thoughts crowd our mind. Our reflections draw us deeper into the mystery of love.

Jesus was well aware of the suffering his Mother endured as she stood beneath that cross. The sharp, two-edged sword predicted by Simeon was penetrating still deeper into her maternal heart.

Jesus had witnessed the pain of separation caused by death, which the widow of Naim suffered when she lost her only son. Listen to the empathy of his loving heart as "The Lord moved with pity upon seeing her and said to her: 'Do not cry' " (Luke 7:11-17). Moved by his merciful compassion he restored life to the widow's son and gave him back to his mother.

Likewise the death of the daughter of Jairus

moved Jesus deeply. Her mother and father stood helplessly by as the little girl of twelve breathed her last. The pain of separation was mirrored on the countenance of Jairus as he begged Jesus with a trembling voice to come to his home. Overwhelmed with compassion Jesus not only went down to his home, but restored his daughter to life.

Scholars are not certain why, at the death of Lazarus, Jesus "was troubled in spirit, moved by the deepest emotions" (John 11:33). Was Jesus angry at the ravages of sin causing death, or was he moved with compassion at the suffering of Martha and Mary in the loss of their beloved brother? Again Jesus used his power over death to alleviate suffering.

On Calvary Jesus accepted the oblation of his Mother. According to the divine plan, Mary was closely associated with the passion and death of her Son. She had given her unconditional 'fiat' and that is why she "stood" near the cross of Jesus.

Mary's suffering was intensified by all the circumstances surrounding his death. She witnessed the barbaric cruelty of the executioners, the flagrant injustice of the judges, the perfidy of his enemies, the desertion by his disciples, the traitorous attitude of the crowd. Those who a few days earlier sang his praises now were clamoring for his death. All this added to the dreadful pain rending her heart.

Jesus was not compelled to pour out every last drop of his blood for our redemption, but his infinite love for each one of us could not be satisfied with anything less than the total gift of himself.

The same is true of Mary, our Mother. Her love for Jesus and for each one of us, her children, is so tremendous that she, like her Son, wanted to give herself completely and entirely. She did not wish to be spared any suffering. This does not imply in any way that Mary was masochistic. Mary loved with a great love, and love must give; in fact, love must give all!

Mary is our exemplar as she stands courageously beneath her Son's deathbed on the cross. By her presence and her attitude she is encouraging us to accept whatever comes our way in union with her Son.

Mary continues her special role beneath the cross of Jesus. As a Mother who loves us, her adopted children, she invites us to come to the cross. She asks us to stand close to her and let the message and the mystery of the cross sink deep into our hearts.

When our cross of suffering seems too much to bear and we are tempted to lay it down, Mary quietly and gently urges us to look up to her Son.

When we are rejected, hurt, misunderstood, and find it hard to forgive, Mary invites us to listen to the insults, the mockery, the blasphemy which is being hurled at her Son. As we listen to this barrage of ridicule and insults, we hear the voice of Jesus loud and clear: "Father, forgive them; they do not know what they are doing" (*Luke 23:34*).

When we are discouraged, disheartened, fearful of the future, all we need do is to look at Mary as she gazes upon Jesus suspended between heaven and earth.

When we are selfish, self-centered, looking after our own interests, or when we become attached to mundane treasures, Mary points to the naked Jesus. He was stripped of everything so that he might give all for our salvation.

When our pride forms a real barrier in reaching out in love toward others, Mary would remind us that Jesus humbly accepted the penalty leveled against him without a word in his own defense.

This is the precise role which Jesus wants his Mother to have in our lives; that is why he gave his Mother to us through St. John at the foot of the cross.

She was his last and greatest treasure on earth, but love must give all! Now that treasure is ours!

Pieta

"There is your son . . . There is your mother."

John 19:26-30

Who of us have not stood in awe and reverence as we contemplated that superb masterpiece of Michelangelo, the Pieta. The creative genius of the artist has captured and immortalized the sixth sorrow to pierce the Immaculate Heart of his Mother. This we commemorate in the thirteenth station.

Michelangelo's creation has been acclaimed as a masterpiece down through the years. It has won the hearts of countless people, not only for its beauty and artistry, but for the message it conveys to us.

Joseph and Nicodemus reverently and lovingly took the body of Jesus off the cross and gently placed it in the waiting arms of his Mother. Mary cradled the lifeless body of her Son and pressed it to her bosom. It was cold and clammy in death and did not respond to her loving embrace.

87

Mary could trace in every wound, in every laceration, the outpouring of Jesus' love in response to the infinite love that the Father had for him. What greater proof do we need of the infinite love that he has for each one of us? Did Jesus himself not say: "There is no greater love than this: to lay down one's life for one's friends" (John 15:13).

We wonder how any mother could bear such inhuman treatment to her son without experiencing bitterness and resentment. Mary accepted it without any rancor. She could do so because she had committed herself totally to God's will, come what may.

By way of application, I am sure that the words of Lamentations could be applied to Mary:

"Come, all you who pass by the way,
   look and see
Whether there is any suffering like my
   suffering
   which has been dealt me" (Lamentations 1:12).

Separation is always painful, but especially for a mother. There are painful partings when close friends move away, when children leave home to take their place in the world, but especially painful is the death of a loved one.

A popular axiom which is displayed in so many strategic places reminds us: "Earth is a continual goodbye; heaven must be an eternal hello."

Mary experienced the pain of separation many times in her life. This separation carried with it greater finality. Yet she experienced peace deep within her. Mary was peaceful because she "knew" that all her Son's suffering was not in vain. In spite of his apparent defeat, it was the greatest victory ever to be achieved in the history of mankind.

Furthermore, Mary was the special temple of the Holy Spirit. The Spirit was able to fill her with his gifts of knowledge and understanding. Deep within her, Mary knew that this was not the end, but only the beginning of a glorious reign for her Son. This was his victory over sin and death.

Jesus had already prepared us for the great triumph which we would enjoy. He explained it in this simple metaphor:

"I tell you truly:
    you will weep and mourn
    while the world rejoices;
    you will grieve for a time,
    but your grief will be turned to joy.
When a woman is in labor
    she is sad that her time has come.
    When she has borne her child,
    she no longer remembers her pain
    for the joy that a man has been born

into the world.
In the same way, you are sad for a time,
    but I shall see you again;
    then your hearts will rejoice
    with a joy no one can take from you"
    (John 16:20-22).

Centuries before, Queen Esther, who was a prophetic image of Mary, prayed earnestly before she delivered her people Israel. Her prayer can well become our own:

"Hear my prayer; have pity on your inheritance and turn our sorrow into joy: thus we shall live to sing praise to your name, O Lord. Do not silence those who praise you" (Esther 4:C 10).

As Mary pressed the lifeless body of her Son to her heart, she must have experienced feelings of great relief. On the cross Jesus said: "Now it is finished" (John 19:30). Mary's heart must have reiterated that same statement with: "Yes, it is done." Her maternal heart must have rejoiced in the knowledge that her children all over the world and for all times were redeemed and would someday enjoy the total union of love with her Son.

How appropriately the words of Isaiah remind us that our earthly sojourn will end in great joy and jubilation.

"Those whom the Lord has ransomed
    will return

and enter Zion singing,
crowned with everlasting joy;
They will meet with joy and gladness,
sorrow and mourning will flee"
(Isaiah 51:11).

Sealed With a Stone

"The women . . . saw the tomb
and how his body was buried."

Luke 23:50-56

If we have gone through the experience of losing in death someone near and dear to us, be it a
mother, father, spouse, or even a close friend,
then we know the pain of separation. There is an
emptiness in our lives; a void which cannot be
easily filled. The loneliness which we experience
is often an abiding pain. As we realize the finality
of death, the pain becomes more acute. We will
never see or share with that person again in this
land of exile.

If this is true of our human relationships, how
much truer it is of the deep, personal relationship
which existed between Jesus and his Mother.
The rich, human love which united them was free
from all the weaknesses and encumbrances which
sinful human nature imposes on our love for
another. Their love for each other had a human as

well as a divine dimension.

When Jesus finally handed over his life to the Father, there must have been some moments of relief for Mary. When Jesus uttered, "It is finished," his Mother must have welcomed the end of his torturous suffering. Then the realization of loss descended upon her. Her Son was gone. Suddenly the world was empty. It was cold, cruel, forbidding.

The pain of separation was not new to Mary. She had experienced it many times in her life. She had to flee with Joseph and the Infant Jesus to a foreign country, Egypt, because Herod was determined to eliminate any threat to his dubious kingship. She must have missed family and friends.

She felt the sharp pain of separation when Jesus was lost in the Temple at the age of twelve. The uncertainty of finding him again intensified the pain.

Who could comprehend the anguish of her maternal heart when the time arrived according to the Father's decree, that Jesus would leave the peaceful confines of his Nazareth home to begin his public ministry? Try to imagine the emptiness in Mary's heart at the vacant place at table, or when she no longer could pray and chant the prayers of her people with Jesus. Gone, too, were the times when they could enjoy the beauty of creation, the provident love of the Father for the birds of the air and the lilies of the field. The sounds which issued from the carpenter's shop were ominously silent; the stillness was haunting.

Here on Calvary's hill Mary did find some comfort in the realization that the apostles were experiencing that same pain of loneliness without their divine Master and that they needed her now more than ever. Her maternal heart reached out to them in loving compassion.

Standing here in the shadow of the cross Mary did find some consolation in the loving concern of the two disciples, Joseph of Arimathaea and Nicodemus, who gently took Jesus' body down from the cross and prepared it for burial. She was pleased with their loving concern poured out upon the beaten and bruised body of her Son.

Mary must have been greatly gratified to witness the love and loyalty showered upon her Son by the holy women who stood courageously beside him throughout his bitter suffering and death. Even in death they did not leave him. "Mary Magdalene and the other Mary remained sitting there, facing the tomb" *(Matthew 27:61)*.

Their tender solicitude must have brought great comfort and joy to her pierced heart; however, all their kindness could not fill the tremendous void in her heart. Her aloneness was unique.

Surely Mary's pain was mitigated by the empathy of the apostles, the disciples and the holy women supporting her in this dreadful hour of separation; furthermore, they were looking to her for comfort and reassurance. What joy comes to a mother's heart when she is needed.

As we contemplate the emptiness, the void, the aloneness which Mary suffered in losing her Son in death, it brings us to a greater appreciation of the treasure which is ours.

Jesus promised: "I will not leave you orphaned; I will come back to you" (John 14:18). Jesus kept that promise in a singular way. He rose from the dead so that he could share with us his risen, exalted, glorified life. He is living with us and within us here and now in our land of exile, and he will continue to live with us in a fuller, richer way for all eternity.

St. Paul asks: "Who will separate us from the love of Christ?" (Romans 8:35). Only one thing: sin. Sin is our malicious rejection of his love.

The punishment for sin is the experience of loneliness, emptiness, the lack of peace and joy, the disillusionment, the ashes of frustration and disappointment.

Mary is the refuge of sinners. She endured this painful experience of losing Jesus so that she might intercede more earnestly for sinners. "Holy Mary, Mother of God pray for us sinners, now and at the hour of our death."

Faith's Reward

"He was seen by five hundred brothers."

I Corinthians 15:1-8

Mary's role in the redemption of the world was singular and gigantic. From the moment of the Annunciation until the last gasp of Jesus on the cross, Mary gave herself without reservation. Mary was single-minded in fulfilling the Father's will. There was never a moment of self-concern or hesitation.

In our prayer let us live with Mary those days which followed the crucifixion. She must have spent much time in prayer after the cruel death of her Son on the cross. Her prayer was mingled with joy and sorrow.

Her joy emanated from her awareness that by his passion and death Jesus had redeemed a world. Another source of her joy was the knowledge that Jesus was faithful to his promises. Earlier Jesus has told his followers:

"The Father loves me for this:
    that I lay down my life
    to take it up again.
No one takes it from me;
    I lay it down freely
I have the power to lay it down
    and I have the power to take it up
    again" *(John 10:17-18)*.

Mary was also aware of the reason Jesus lay down his life. He loved us so much he wanted to share his divine life with us. He explained why he came into the world, thus:

". . . I came that they might have life
    and have it to the full" *(John 10:10)*.

Not only Mary's joy, but her sorrow, is understandable. In her humanness she experienced the pain of separation. How she must have relived those treasured experiences at Nazareth during those thirty precious years. How she would like to have prolonged them into an eternity.

In all of this Mary's faith was unshakeable. If her Son promised to take up his life again, Mary was convinced he would do so. She might not have been certain just how he would do so.

The words of her Son re-echoed in her heart. How often he asked for faith in him and how pleased he was when he found that faith. Mary might have recalled the specific incident when Jesus said to the anguished father: "Fear is useless; what is needed is trust . . ." *(Luke 8:50).* Mary passed these hours in trusting prayer.

One of the most common and least contested traditions surrounding the life of Jesus is the belief that he first appeared to his Mother on Resurrection day. It is true that there is no mention of this fact in Sacred Scripture. St. Ignatius says: "Though this is not mentioned explicitly in the Scripture it must be considered as stated when Scripture says that he appeared to many others" *(I Corinthians 15:1-8).*

Nor are we inclined to question this appearance of Jesus to his Mother. One of the reasons why it may not be mentioned in Sacred Scripture is the futility which the writers might have experienced in trying to describe verbally such a mystical phenomenon as the appearance of Jesus in his glorified, exalted, risen life.

Mary's cooperation in his redemptive work was so wholehearted that Jesus could not let it go unnoticed. Furthermore her entire life was one continuous dying to self and a total surrender in love to God's inscrutable plan.

The many appearances of Jesus after the Resurrection can be classified into two categories. First, he appeared to all his family and friends who were loyal to him to the end. He wanted to bring comfort and consolation and to share his joy with them. Secondly, he appeared to the apostles and disciples, not only to reassure them of his loving concern, but to prove the authenticity of his rising.

Humanly speaking Jesus' first thought must have been for his Mother. How eager he was to reveal himself to her. How dearly he loved her.

Mary's joy must have been beyond comprehension. She was overjoyed at seeing her Son again and realized more fully that Jesus was closer to her in his risen life than he was before his death. There would be no more separations.

Mary also rejoiced in her Son's glory. He had finished the work the Father had given him to do and was now in his glory continuing his redemptive work until every creature is united with him in glory.

Mary's joy was augmented because she understood the comfort and consolation, the happiness and joy, which his rising would bring not only to his contemporaries, but to all persons yet to be born.

Mary rejoiced because she foresaw the reassurance and hope which his rising would bring to us here and now in this land of exile. What a guarantee it brings us of our eternal destiny and of our own resurrection with him.

Gathered in My Name

"Together they devoted themselves
to constant prayer."

Acts 1:12-14

Christianity is essentially communitarian.
Jesus founded his Church as a family, as a community. The people of God who are members of
his Church form his Body in the world today.

We became members of his Church through
our Baptism as Paul reminds us: "It was in one
Spirit that all of us, whether Jew or Greek, slave
or free, were baptized into one body. All of us
have been given to drink of the one Spirit" (I Corinthians 12:13f).

The binding force uniting us in genuine Christian community is the divine life of Jesus surging
through, animating, vivifying every member of his
Body. ". . . And is not the bread we break a sharing in the body of Christ? Because the loaf of
bread is one, we, many though we are, are one
body, for we partake of the one loaf" (I Corin

thians 10:16).

At every Eucharistic celebration we pray for the unity of this Body. "May all of us who share in the body and blood of Christ be brought together in unity by the Holy Spirit" *(Eucharistic Prayer II).*

Prayer, be it eucharistic, private or common, is the unifying and binding force in Christian community. Here again Mary is our exemplar.

After the Ascension of Jesus into heaven, the disciples returned to the Upper Room to begin a ten-day period of prayer. Luke's statement is rather brief, but we can read much between the lines. "Entering the city, they went to the upstairs room where they were staying . . . . Together they devoted themselves to constant prayer. There were some women in their company, and Mary the Mother of Jesus, and his brothers" *(Acts 1:13ff).*

In this scene Mary teaches us a good deal about prayer. At the wedding in Cana of Galilee, Jesus proved the intercessory power of Mary's prayer. Now she joins with this little Messianic community to implore God to pour down his Spirit upon them.

Mary had been overshadowed by the Holy Spirit. From the moment of her own conception she was the temple of the Holy Spirit. During her maturing years, the Holy Spirit had formed her mentality, her attitudes and her vision to be in perfect union with the will of God. He had enkindled in her virginal heart his divine love. She enjoyed his precious gifts of wisdom, knowledge and understanding. He had prepared and strengthened her for every trial.

Gathered here with the people her Son had chosen and the ones she loved so dearly, she interceded for them again. She begged the Father to pour out his Spirit upon them so that they might be better prepared to accept the challenging ministry with which Jesus charged them.

Jesus had promised: "I will ask the Father and he will give you another Paraclete — to be with you always" (John 14:16). In her ardent prayer, Mary must have reminded Jesus of this promise.

Those ten days of prayer transformed the disciples and made them receptive to the power and presence of the Holy Spirit when he came upon them at Pentecost.

Mary's prayer did not stop with the descent of the Holy Spirit, however. Today she is rightly called the Mother of the Church because her intercession continues for all her children and will continue to the end of time. Thus she is fulfilling her role as Mother.

Mary is also our exemplar in shared prayer or communal prayer. She shared in the prayer of the disciples; also, she shared her prayer with them.

Her presence was a prayer. Her own deep faith was reflected in all her attitudes and actions.

Her countenance radiated the joy and peace of her heart. Her love for God and for others beamed forth constantly.

Together with the disciples she pondered, reflected and shared the work which Jesus gave them to do.

United in mind and heart, they prayed for strength and enlightenment to understand just what God's will for them was.

They recognized their own poverty and knew that without Jesus they could do nothing. Mary must have shared her own feelings about her inadequacy when she was asked to become the Mother of Jesus. No doubt she also reminded them of the words of her own canticle: "God who is mighty has done great things for me, holy is his name" *(Luke 1:49)*.

Once again in our day, we are discovering the unifying and healing power of shared or communal prayer. By sharing her own personal experience of Jesus with the first Christian community, Mary encouraged them and drew them into this communal prayer posture.

Through her powerful intercession, may Mary also bring us into a loving Christian community founded on love and formed through prayer.

Sharing a Mother

"God sent forth his Son born of a woman."

Galatians 4:4

How appropriately we begin the new calendar year by celebrating the Solemnity of Mary, the Mother of God!

"Yes, God so loved the world that he gave his only Son, that whoever believes in him may not die, but may have eternal life" (John 3:16). This brief statement is a mysterious, but powerful manifestation of God's infinite love for us. He gave us his Son in a unique way.

In giving us the greatest of all his gifts, his only Son, God provided a Mother for him that he might enter into our world. Our loving Father called Mary to be the Mother of his Son. He preserved her from all sin that she might cradle the sinless one in her womb.

Mary's sinlessness gave her a great capacity to love. Her sinlessness removed all obstacles such as pride, self-centeredness, insecurity, doubt, fear and the host of barriers which prevent us from loving completely and without reservation.

Such is the mystery of God's incomprehensible love. Mary responded to that outpouring with every fibre of her being. She wanted to make herself receptive to that divine love. She wanted to become a perfect temple for the Savior which she was to conceive by the power of the Holy Spirit.

How incongruous is God's love! He wanted his Son to come into this world like any other child — fragile, needy, dependent, helpless, vulnerable, trusting.

"God sent forth his Son, born of a woman" (*Galatians* 4:4). The Son of God is also the Son of Mary. She is the Mother of God, yet like her Child and because of her Child, she is poor, dependent, vulnerable.

The message is plain. God comes into our world in weakness. His power is love, exemplified in his Mother's love. Redemption is accomplished through love, and love is always vulnerable.

Because of her great love, Mary had to respond to God in love to give herself totally to him. What more complete oblation than her words: "I am the servant of the Lord. Let it be done to me as you say" (*Luke* 1:38).

Love asks even more. We cannot be satisfied in merely reaching out to give ourselves to God in love, we must reach out on the horizontal level as well. Mary did just that. She was the first Christ-bearer. She brought Jesus to the world.

She presented Jesus to the shepherds who had responded in courage, faith and simplicity to the angelic invitation. Later she presented him to the astrologers who had come from the East; then to Simeon and Anna who had prayerfully awaited his coming. Finally Mary presented her Son to a world awaiting a Redeemer.

Now, as our Mother, Mary teaches us how to bring Jesus to the world.

We must, first of all, receive Jesus into our own lives. He must be the center of our whole life. We must receive him with faith, with poverty of spirit, with simplicity, with courage and above all with love.

When Jesus becomes the first priority in our lives, then like Mary we will be able to present him to the world in which we live, move and have our being.

We can nurture the growth of Jesus in others by a deep, loving concern for their welfare. That concern makes us vulnerable to disappointment, misunderstanding and hurt but we can be redeemed through that pain. Each one of us is needy. We must be saved. We need the help of others to bring us fully alive.

Again Mary shows us the way. "Mary treasured all these things and reflected on them in her heart" *(Luke 2:19)*.

As we go about our daily round of events, we too must reflect on what God is telling us. He speaks to us through the people who come into our lives and through the events around us. Like Mary we can develop a continuing attitude of listening to what God is telling us through these persons and events. He is guiding and nurturing growth in us through those he sends into our lives so that we, in turn, will be better able to draw others into a deeper spiritual maturity.

As we become aware of his mysterious working in our lives, we will with the simplicity and courage of the shepherds, glorify and praise God for the outpouring of his love upon us. He not only gave us his own divine Son, he gave us a Mother.

Non-Stop Flight to Heaven

". . . in Christ all will come to life again,
but each one in proper order."

I Corinthians 15:20-28

If you were to visit Jerusalem today you would find, close to the Cenacle where Jesus instituted the Holy Eucharist the night before he died, a large neo-Romanesque church called the Church of the Dormition, Mary's "falling asleep." This Church looks somewhat like a medieval fortress. It is cared for by the Benedictines. In the crypt is a beautiful statue our Blessed Mother lying in the peaceful slumber of death.

If you were to proceed along the route Jesus took on the way to Gethsemane, you would discover, very close to the Garden of Olives, the Church of the Assumption.

Mary was buried here according to tradition. From this tomb she was taken straight into heaven because she was without sin; hence, she did not have to suffer the consequences of sin which is the corruption of the flesh.

We depend upon tradition to locate these sites. They may not be accurate. However, we do believe that Mary was assumed body and soul into heaven. This has always been the teaching of the Church.

In 1950 our Holy Father, Pope Pius XII, declared formally to the world the beautiful dogma of Mary's Assumption into heaven. The definition of this doctrine was proclaimed in these words: "We proclaim and define it to be a dogma revealed by God that the immaculate mother of God, Mary ever Virgin, when the course of her earthly life was finished, was taken up 'body and soul' into heavenly glory."

We look upon death as the "wages of sin." If Adam had not sinned, we would have entered heaven, not through the doors of death, but through a sort of gentle sleep.

By way of a special dispensation, the fruits of the redemption were pre-applied to Mary so that she would be conceived without the slightest effects of sin. Furthermore her soul was preserved from the stain of any sin through the special power of God. Her mind, heart and soul were always in perfect accord with God's divine plan. Her life was a continual dying to self so that she could give herself without reservation to the Father's will.

Mary's total surrender to God began when

she proclaimed so eloquently at the time of the Annunciation: "I am the servant of the Lord. Let it be done to me as you say" *(Luke 1:38)*.

Mary never withdrew any part of that commitment. In fact, each day was a deeper, fuller renewal of that surrender to God.

Mary's immediate resurrection occurred because during her life on earth she had died totally to self and had given herself completely to God.

Resurrection is a series of yes's to the loving plan of our Father. Our own resurrection began at the moment of our Baptism. In Baptism we are incorporated into the Body of Christ. We participate in the trinitarian life. St. Peter says we become "sharer in the glory that is to be revealed" *(I Peter 5:1)*.

When we were baptized, we also became the temples of the Holy Spirit. St. Paul asks: "Are you not aware that you are the temple of God, and that the Spirit of God dwells in you? . . . the temple of God is holy, and you are that temple" *(I Corinthians 3:16f)*.

The Holy Spirit abides with us and within us with his dynamic presence and power. That same Spirit overshadowed Mary and made her his very special temple — his vessel of election.

The Holy Spirit begins his process of purifying and sanctifying us at the moment of Baptism. Even though we are self-centered and sinful people, the glory of the resurrection is already being effected in us by the Holy Spirit.

If the resurrection has already begun in us — with all our humanness and waywardness — how much more effectively did the resurrection take place in Mary who was free of every encumbrance of sin! Already this chaste and pure Virgin of Nazareth was closely united with God because of her total surrender in love to him.

Of all the members of the Body of Christ, who but Mary enjoys the highest oneness with Jesus? The Church professes that Mary received a conglorification: body, soul and spirit, with Jesus. This is her assumption into heaven.

As Mary intimately shared in the life, suffering and death of her Son, so the Church believes she shares now in his glory.

St. Paul teaches: "Just as in Adam all die, so in Christ all will come to life again, but each one in proper order: Christ the first fruits and then, at his coming, all those who belong to him" (*I Corinthians 15:22f*). Who belonged to him more intimately, more perseveringly than did his Mother? Mary belongs to Jesus as Mother to Son, as the living member of his Body closest in relation to him, the head.

Mary's assumption into heaven gives us the reassurance of our own resurrection. It reminds us that she is also our Mother and hence is maternally concerned about our resurrection and life with her and her Son for all eternity. That is why we pray earnestly each day: "Holy Mary, Mother of God, pray for us sinners now and at the hour of our death."

Mary, Queen of Heaven

". . . those he justified he in turn glorified."

Romans 8:28-35

Sometime ago, on a certain popular television program, a woman would be selected and made "Queen for a Day." On this day of her reign she was entertained in royal style. Gifts and honors were heaped upon her in true secular fashion. This program reminded me that we Christians too have a Queen.

Our Queen is not merely a queen for a day, but for all eternity; not only a queen over a particular family or a people, but over all nations and peoples. Our Queen's reign is not one of invested power, but one of love, the love of a Mother. Our Queen is the Mother of Jesus and our Mother — the Queen of heaven and earth.

Mary is the Queen of all the angels and saints in heaven. She is also Queen of all her children on pilgrimage here on this earth.

In its liturgy the Church applies the words of

St. Paul to Mary: "Those he predestined he like-wise called; those he called he also justified; and those he justified he in turn glorified" *(Romans 8:30).*

How aptly these words apply to Mary our Mother and Queen. Certainly she was called by God to a very special vocation. In order that she might be prepared to be the Mother of his Son, God pre-applied the fruits of the redemption to her so that she was already justified. After completing her earthly sojourn, Mary was taken into heaven where she finds glory in fulfilling her mission to the world.

Mary is glorified in heaven along with her Son, Jesus. Of what does Mary's glory consist? Mary's glory, like that of Jesus, is not static enjoyment of a heavenly reward. No, her glory consists in being present to Jesus and through him to our heavenly Father by the overshadowing of the Holy Spirit.

She is present to us through the immense "oneness" that she enjoys with the Blessed Trinity. How effectively the prayer of Jesus in his Last Discourse in the Upper Room was fulfilled in his Mother:

". . . that all may be one
as you, Father, are in me, and I in you;
I pray that they may be [one] in us,
that the world may believe that you

sent me . . . .
Father, all those you gave me
I would have in my company where I am
to see this glory of mine
which is your gift to me." *(John 17:21-24)*

Mary is present to the Holy Trinity. She is also universally present to every human being. Because of her great love, Mary wants to share abundantly with others the goodness and love which God has given her.

The greater the gift of love we receive, the more we wish to share with others. Upon entering into her glory in heaven, Mary was full of grace. The angel Gabriel declared her full of grace when the Holy Spirit overshadowed her and when she surrendered completely in loving service to her Lord in humble lowliness *(Luke 1:38)*.

Mary continued to grow in love of God as she permitted God's love in her to make her more open, more present and more generous in loving service to others. Surely she must have grown in love as she served her Son at Nazareth for thirty years! At the foot of the cross how that grace must have reached its fullness. How she wanted to reach out to every person in the whole world so that the blood of her Son might not be poured out in vain.

As her mission of loving service continues, she becomes more and more our Queen and Mother.

Mary's presence to Jesus in love means that she has his own mind. Jesus living in her makes her want to surrender herself continually in loving service to others.

We say that Jesus is in his glory and that his glory lies in fulfilling his role as mediator by interceding continuously for us. Mary, who is so intimately united with her Son, is interceding along with him for each one of us, her children.

While on earth Mary lived only for Jesus. How much more does she want to bring everyone of us to him in heaven! This means that in the teaching of the Church, Mary can and does intercede for us when we pray to her. It means that Mary is now living with full consciousness, memory and understanding of our needs here on earth. Mary reaches out in love to all of us, especially to the most needy.

St. Paul could say: "I have made myself all things to all men in order to save at least some of them" (*I Corinthians 9:22*). How much greater is the loving concern and zeal of Mary for each one of her children.

St. Paul also says: "You are my children, and you put me back in labor pains until Christ is formed in you" (*Galatians 4:19*). Mary, who in her earthly life gave birth to Jesus, wants continually in her glory to form Jesus in all the children Jesus entrusted to her from his deathbed on the cross.

The Church is very much aware of this mission of Mary; hence in Vatican Council II it called Mary the Mother of the Church.

Among all Christians who have departed this life and are now enjoying life eternal, Mary is the most "possessed" by God's spirit of love, the most "full of grace." She is more present to us than all the angels and saints.

Mother of the Church

"There is your Mother."

John 19:25-27

Our Holy Father is truly the Shepherd of the People of God. Like the Good Shepherd whom he represents he leads us "in verdant pastures . . . He guides me in right paths" *(Psalm 23)*.

In those critical post-conciliar days of renewal, Pope Paul VI, as our Shepherd, restated a truth which is a source of much hope and encouragement to us on our pilgrimage through life.

In the midst of some challenging and confusing theories about the precise role of Mary in the economy of salvation, Pope Paul VI joyfully and emphatically proclaimed Mary to be the 'Mother of the Church.' The Holy Father conferred this title 'Mother of the Church' upon Mary in his closing allocution at the end of the third session of the Second Vatican Council (November 21, 1964). We the Church have a Mother.

In the conciliar document, Dogmatic Constitution on the Church, the Bishops taught this same truth without actually conferring this title on our Blessed Mother.

They said: "She is endowed with the supreme office and dignity of being the Mother of the Son of God. As a result she is also the favorite daughter of the Father and the temple of the Holy Spirit."

And the Bishops' statement continued: "Indeed she is clearly the mother of the members of Christ . . . since she cooperated out of love so that there might be born in the Church the faithful who are members of Christ the Head" (Par. 53).

This is not an empty title, nor is it a poetic or pious expression. It is not merely a title of honor. It is a truth in the real sense of the term. The Holy Father was verbalizing what the Bishops taught about Mary in this document.

According to God's divine plan, Mary fulfills a very special role of motherhood in the universal Church.

Mary is the Mother of that part of the Church which we call the Church Triumphant. Mary is the Mother of the angels and saints in heaven, because she is the Mother of Jesus who is their Lord and King.

With a loving motherly concern, Mary glorifies God with all the angels and saints. At the same time she is mindful of all of us still on our pilgrimage here on earth. In heaven Mary joins that band of powerful intercessors in reaching out in loving concern for all of us, a pilgrim people.

Heaven is a state of perfect love. Mary, along with the angels and saints, enjoys the infinite out-pouring of God's love for them, and needs to find someone with whom she can share that love. We are loved and supported by Mary and by all the angels and saints who she leads in their apos-tolate of loving concern for us.

Secondly, Mary is the Mother of the Church Suffering. According to current theological thought purgatory is that state where a person continues to die to self-centeredness and continues to sur-render in love to God. It is a state where a person experiences the pain of separation, but it is also a state of great joy.

Persons still going through this process of dying to self are lovingly concerned about all those who they left behind. In dying to self they must reach out in healing love to others. Their special mission is to love and pray for those of us still on pilgrimage.

These persons are very dear to Mary because they love her Son with such an ardent love. She leads them in their mission of reaching out in love for us. This love is expressed principally in prayer. Mary not only encourages these persons in purga-tory to pray for us, but she lovingly leads them in their powerful intercession for us wayfarers.

Thirdly, Mary is also the Mother of the Church Militant, the Pilgrim Church on its way to the Father. We, the pilgrim Church, have a special claim on Mary since Jesus confirmed her motherhood from his deathbed on the cross: "There is your Mother" *(John 19:27)*.

Mary is very much aware of the joys and successes, the struggles and sorrows which beset us as we journey heavenward. Her maternal heart is always solicitous about our spiritual well-being.

Mary's lifestyle here on earth is a model for us to follow. Amid poverty and rejection, she remained ever faithful to her total commitment to the Father. Even though she could not understand clearly the purpose of these trials and tribulations, she never once wavered in her 'Fiat.' She meant it when she said: "I am the servant of the Lord. Let it be done to me as you say" *(Luke 1:38)*.

Mary shows us the way by her life of prayer. Her prayer was contemplative, as Luke says: "Mary treasured all these things and reflected on them in her heart." And again: "His Mother meanwhile kept all these things in memory" *(Luke 2:19&51)*.

During her hours of prayer Mary discovered God's will for her. When she was absorbed in prayer, the Holy Spirit enlightened, guided, strengthened, consoled and comforted her so that her attitude could always be: 'Here I am Lord, what is it you want?'

Mary's prayer was always a joyous hymn of praise and thanksgiving to God. Her Magnificat was only one expression of the joy which filled her heart.

Next to the gift of himself in the Person of Jesus, what more could our loving Father have given us than the Mother of his Son? As the Mother of the Church she is our Mother, and as our Mother, she is "a sign of sure hope and solace for the pilgrim People of God" *(Ibid Par. 68)*.

TO COMFORT AND CONFRONT
Biblical Reflections   2.95

Kenneth Overberg, S.J. We are challenged today through the timelessness of Scripture to meet the needs of our evolving world and take action. Individuals will find fresh insight and questions for private prayer. Communities and prayer groups will find stimulating starting points for shared prayer.

WHOLENESS
The Legacy of Jesus   2.50

Adolfo Quezada presents practical and spiritual perspectives to those seeking purpose and meaning in their lives. He faces the reality that we are all broken by the impact of suffering and torn by the pull of distractions. He offers hope and direction toward a more abundant life.

PRESENCE THROUGH THE WORD   2.50

Sr. Evelyn Ann Schumacher, O.S.F. Personal intimacy with the Father, the Son and the Holy Spirit is meant for every Christian. Experience of that presence is attainable in our lives as we trace the ancient quest of others through the pages of Scripture.

SPIRITUAL DIRECTION
Contemporary Readings   5.95

Edited by Kevin Culligan, O.C.D. The revitalized ministry of spiritual direction is one of the surest signs of renewal in today's Church. In this book seventeen leading writers and spiritual directors discuss history, meaning, demands and practice of this ministry. Readers of the book should include not just a spiritual elite, but the entire Church — men and women, clergy and laity, members of religious communities.

PRAYER:
The Eastern Tradition   2.95

Andrew Ryder, S.C.J. In the East there is no sharp distinction between prayer and theology. Far from being divorced they are seen as supporting and completing each other. One is impossible without the other. Theology is not an end in itself, but rather a means, a way to union with God.

THE RETURNING SUN
Hope for a Broken World   2.50

George A. Maloney, S.J. In this collection of meditations, the author draws on his own experiences rooted in Eastern Christianity to aid the reader to enter into the world of the "heart." It is hoped that through contemplation of this material he/she will discover the return of the inextinguishable Sun of the universe, Jesus Christ, in a new and more experiential way.

LIVING HERE AND HEREAFTER
Christian Dying,
Death and Resurrection   2.95

Msgr. David E. Rosage. The author offers great comfort to us by dispelling our fears and anxieties about our life after this earthly sojourn. Based on God's Word as presented in Sacred Scripture, these brief daily meditations help us understand more clearly and deeply the meaning of suffering and death.

PRAYING WITH SCRIPTURE
IN THE HOLY LAND
Daily Meditations With the Risen Jesus   3.50

Msgr. David E. Rosage. Herein is offered a daily meeting with the Risen Jesus in those Holy Places which He sanctified by His human presence. Three hundred and sixty-five scripture texts are selected and blended with the pilgrimage experiences of the author, a retreat master, and well-known writer on prayer.

DISCERNMENT:
Seeking God in Every Situation   3.50

Rev. Chris Aridas. "Many Christians struggle with ways to seek, know and understand God's plan for their lives. This book is prayerful, refreshing and very practical for daily application. It is one to be read and used regularly, not just read" *(Ray Roh, O.S.B.).*

A DESERT PLACE   2.50

Adolfo Quezada. "The author speaks of the desert place deep within, where one can share the joy of the Lord's presence, but also the pain of the nights of our own faithlessness" *(Pecos Benedictine).*

MOURNING: THE HEALING JOURNEY   2.95

Rev. Kenneth J. Zanca. Comfort for those who have lost a loved one. Out of the grief suffered in the loss of both parents within two months, this young priest has written a sensitive, sympathetic yet humanly constructive book to help others who have lost loved ones. This is a book that might be given to the newly bereaved.

THE BORN-AGAIN CATHOLIC   3.95

Albert H. Boudreau. This book presents an authoritative imprimatur treatment of today's most interesting religious issue. The author, a Catholic layman, looks at Church tradition past and present and shows that the born-again experience is not only valid, but actually is Catholic Christianity at its best. The exciting experience is not only investigated, but the reader is guided into revitalizing his or her own Christian experience. The informal style, colorful personal experiences, and helpful diagrams make this book enjoyable and profitable reading.

WISDOM INSTRUCTS HER CHILDREN
The Power of the Spirit and the Word   3.50

John Randall, S.T.D. The author believes that now is God's time for "wisdom." Through the Holy Spirit, "power" has become much more accessible in the Church. Wisdom, however, lags behind and the result is imbalance and disarray. The Spirit is now seeking to pour forth a wisdom we never dreamed possible. This outpouring could lead us into a new age of Jesus Christ! This is a badly needed, most important book, not only for the Charismatic Renewal, but for the whole Church.

DISCOVERING
PATHWAYS TO PRAYER   2.95

Msgr. David E. Rosage. Following Jesus was never meant to be dull, or worse, just duty-filled. Those who would aspire to a life of prayer and those who have already begun, will find this book amazingly thorough in its scripture-punctuated approach.

    "A simple but profound book which explains the many ways and forms of prayer by which the person hungering for closer union with God may find him" *(Emmanuel Spillane, O.C.S.O., Abbot, Our Lady of the Holy Trinity Abbey, Huntsville, Utah).*

GRAINS OF WHEAT   2.95

Kelly B. Kelly. This little book of words received in prayer is filled with simple yet often profound leadings, exhortations and encouragement for daily living. Within the pages are insights to help one function as a Christian, day by day, minute by minute.

BREAD FOR THE EATING   2.95

Kelly B. Kelly. Sequel to the popular *Grains of Wheat,* this small book of words received in prayer draws the reader closer to God through the imagery of wheat being processed into bread. The author shares her love of the natural world.

DESERT SILENCE:
A Way of Prayer for an Unquiet Age   2.50

Alan J. Placa and *Brendan Riordan.* The pioneering efforts of the men and women of the early church who went out into the desert to find union with the Lord has relevance for those of us today who are seeking the pure uncluttered desert place within to have it filled with the loving silence of God's presence.

LIVING FLAME PRESS
Box 74, Locust Valley, N.Y. 11560

QUANTITY

_____	Wholeness: The Legacy of Jesus — 2.50
_____	Presence Through the Word — 2.50
_____	To Comfort and Confront — 2.95
_____	Spiritual Direction — 5.95
_____	The Returning Sun — 2.50
_____	Prayer: the Eastern Tradition — 2.95
_____	Living Here and Hereafter — 2.95
_____	Praying With Scripture in the Holy Land — 3.50
_____	Discernment — 3.50
_____	A Desert Place — 2.50
_____	Mourning: The Healing Journey — 2.95
_____	The Born-Again Catholic — 3.95
_____	Wisdom Instructs Her Children — 3.50
_____	Discovering Pathways to Prayer — 2.95
_____	Grains of Wheat — 2.95
_____	Bread for the Eating — 2.95
_____	Desert Silence — 2.50
_____	Who Is This God You Pray To? — 2.95
_____	Union With the Lord in Prayer — 1.50
_____	Attaining Spiritual Maturity — 1.50
_____	Praying With Mary — 2.95
_____	Linger With Me — 3.50
_____	Book of Revelation — 2.50
_____	Seeking Purity of Heart — 2.50
_____	To Live as Jesus Did — 2.95

NAME_____

ADDRESS _____

CITY _____ STATE _____ ZIP_____

Payment enclosed. Kindly include $.70 postage and handling on orders up to $5; $1.00 on orders up to $10; more than $10 but less than $50 add 10% of total; over $50 add 8% of total. Canadian residents add 20% exchange rate, plus postage and handling.